Extraordinary Adventures of An Ordinary Man

Determination, Creativity
and Love for Country

JOHN GULLO

WITH BRIDGET COOK-BURCH

FOREWORD BY THURL BAILEY
FORMER NBA BASKETBALL STAR

Extraordinary Adventures of An Ordinary Man
Determination, Creativity and Love for Country

Inspired Legacy Publishing is a division of (DBA) Inspired Legacy, LIC
PO Box 900816
Sandy UT 84090-0816.

Disclaimer

This is a true memoir. The stories, language, and reflections in these pages are told exactly as John lived them. Growing up in Buffalo meant being surrounded by rough company, sharp humor, and sometimes crude realities. Over time, John became more of a polished professional, an entrepreneur, a philanthropist, and a leader in both business and sport—but he never stopped speaking plainly. Some readers will laugh. Others may bristle.

Be aware. *All* of it is here because it is true. It's how he built empires and legacies, his way. And a memoir of John could never be complete without his real, raw, and honest communication.

Paperback ISBN: 979-8-9956017-0-8
Hardback ISBN: 979-8-9956017-1-5

What People Are Saying

"John Gullo is a unique person and friend. His book is very inspirational, and it will provide motivation to many entrepreneurs, fathers, grandfathers, students, teachers, and more. I recommend reading, digesting and comparing John's story to your own story. Then, reading it again. It's worth it."

—Tom Mueller

24-year Burger King Veteran, Former President and COO, Wendy's International, Inc.

"This is a delightful read, filled with humor and honesty, life's disappointments and successes, mistakes made and wisdom gained. If everyone followed John's "Lessons to Live By," what an amazing world it would be!"

—Fran Myer

Author and 2018 Pickleball Hall of Fame Inductee

"I found it to be beautifully written and engaging throughout. The book is a fascinating insight into the formation of John's strong character, his willingness to take risks for the betterment of himself and others, and his genuinely warm heart... His story is inspiring, and the book is full of meaningful life lessons that resonate long after reading."

—Marsha Freso

USAP former Director of Referees and Ambassador

"John's story was very honest and inspiring. His ideas and creativity shone throughout his life, from saving money to buy Christmas presents for his family at a young age to the Rockin' 4th celebrations. The life lessons at the end of each chapter cause you to reflect on his experiences."

—Leslie Hooks

Family Friend

"It is a fun, engaging read that was truly hard to put down. Even ten years after meeting him, I realized my knowledge of his life was just the tip of the iceberg. The more I read, the more the word WOW crept in... In my mind and my heart, the title should actually be The Extraordinary Adventures of an Extraordinary Man. Thank you, John Gullo, for all you are and all you've done and all you have yet to do."

—Nora Chetterbock

Pickleball Enthusiast

"As a fellow entrepreneur and friend of John Gullo, I devoured this raw memoir... That same fire once got him in trouble, but became rocket fuel for his empire and his drive to lift others. Thurl Bailey's foreword nails it: an ordinary man turned adversity into generosity and legacy. Street-to-boardroom wisdom every founder needs."

—Mark Stiegemeier

World Freestyle Skiing Champion, Business Founder, and Technology Inventor

---

"This book was a joy to read, and I easily and eagerly read each chapter, looking forward to the life lessons John would share. I loved how each chapter of his life began with a powerful quote!
I see this book as a great leadership book! John's life experiences are disclosed in a chronological way and each chapter was an opportunity to learn more about this extraordinary man. I feel privileged to call John Gullo my friend!"

—Pat Nissan

MST Marriage and Family Therapist

"What an outstanding journey! There are so many life lessons and experiences that can assist others along their own journey in this book. I think the book could be in the self-help section.
I'm anxious to get a copy in the hands of a few of our kids who will definitely learn from both John's mistakes and his massive successes. What a great example of a "hand up" not a "hand out!" Thank you, John, for being such a great guy and such a fantastic inspiration and example!"

—Leesa Clark-Price

SR. VP Statue of Responsibility Foundation

Dedication

This book is dedicated to fathers. I didn't grow up with a father-figure, all the way from the age of six until fifteen. Without such a role model, I was definitely headed in the *wrong* direction. When my mother remarried, Red came into my life. I was a rebellious kid who made one huge mistake, and Red turned it into my greatest life lesson.

Red became "Dad," and I learned from him that truth, honesty, and humility are the foundation of character.

In writing this book, I hope to inspire other men to excel at life's responsibilities and great opportunities, and the women who read it to know what to value and look for in a partner, as well as hold precious in themselves.

Table of Contents

Foreword
"With Great Power..."

by "Big T" Thurl Bailey

Former NBA superstar (1983–1999), keynote, singer, songwriter, author & actor

Just by picking up this book, you're about to be plunged into another world, where you have an opportunity to look at life, love, and leadership in a much different way than you've ever known—through the eyes of an ordinary man who's lived an extraordinary life... and one who has deeply affected mine.

Why is this important? Growing up in a high-needs community, my mom didn't give me the chance to forget where I came from. She used to put her fist right under my chin and say, "Thurl, don't you ever forget!"

Forget the neighborhood?

Forget the struggle?

Forget the ones who carried you here?

Not a chance. I carried an unspoken promise deep inside me—a kind of inner agreement with myself: If I ever made something of my life, I'd go back to my neighborhood. Not to show off. Not to escape my roots. But to lift someone else. I didn't just want to make it out. I wanted to make it matter.

Years later, when I reached a certain level of professional recognition, what some call "high profile," I felt the weight that came with it. Being a professional athlete changes how people look at you. Sure, I'd always stood out—literally—just because I was so tall. Then, as I got better at professional basketball, I began to stand out simply because I was Black and successful. And let's be honest—there's a lot of narrative around that combination. People make assumptions. They project ideas onto you.

Yet that Spider-Man quote comes to mind: "With great power comes great responsibility." Corny as it sounds, it's real—if that's how you're built. Not everybody takes that on. Yet it matters how you show up. And plenty of people make it big... and forget where they came from. They lose track of the neighborhoods, the struggles, and the people who fought to give them a shot.

That promise I made as a kid stayed with me. I had a responsibility to show up, not just in arenas and locker rooms, but in communities—especially for kids who didn't see many people who looked like them doing what I was doing. I felt called to be visible—not for ego, but for example. Like an incredible ball player, "Dr. J", had been for me.

That's why I've always said yes to a lot of charity events.

One of those events changed my life.

There was a silent auction where I put up the prize: a day-long basketball clinic for 15 kids. Nothing fancy. A few drills, some scrimmage, and a pep talk.

And that's where John Gullo came in.

John bid on the package and won. But if you know John, you know the man can't stop at "just a clinic." He doesn't think small. I learned quickly that he never does the bare minimum. Instead of 15 kids, he turned it into a full-blown event at the Youth Impact Center in Ogden. He filled the gym with 150 kids, music, energy, and opportunity. I ran the camp, spent the day with the kids, and later spoke at a fundraiser for his foundation.

That day wasn't just a job or an appearance. It was the start of something much bigger. You see, John never forgot where he came from. He never lost track of the struggles of the streets, nor the people who fight to give kids a shot.

I have to say now that I believe that auction, that event was meant to happen. Like-hearted people find each other. Our paths were different, but we had some unique similarities, like coming from the streets. Our values matched: We both believe success only matters if it's shared.

Over time, John and I built something rare: a friendship based on mutual respect and genuine love. Not because we needed anything from each other, but because we recognized something in each other. That need to help kids intertwined our hearts, our families, and our purpose.

I've always been intrigued by John's business mind—sharp, bold, visionary. He built the American Dream Foundation from the ground up, not by talking about giving back, but by living it. And that drew me in.

To know John is to know he's not always gentle around the edges. He's tough. He's direct. He doesn't waste words. But under that steel exterior is a fiercely loyal heart. Honestly? He's helped me through some of the hardest moments of my life. There were times—deeply difficult times—when I leaned on him. And he showed up every time. No spotlight. No fanfare. No "you owe me." Just there. The kind of friend you can count on one hand. Priceless.

John also opened a few unexpected doors in my life. I worked with him on his concerts with guys like Billy Dean, Neal McCoy, and Colin Raye. I even got to record with Neal on one of my albums! While people are often surprised that I love country music as much as the next guy (or as much as John!), real country is all about storytelling. And storytelling—about struggle, hope, redemption—well, that's universal.

Music isn't the only thing John and I bonded over. There's philanthropy. There's faith. And believe it or not, pickleball.

Yeah, pickleball.

John is the father of pro pickleball. He didn't just teach my family and me to play; he saw the potential of pickleball long before it exploded into a national and now international phenomenon! That's how his mind works. He sees things most people miss. And I've learned, over the years, to pay attention to people like him.

Now, as you open these pages, you're stepping into a story that's as bold and unapologetic as the man himself. John doesn't sugarcoat life. He doesn't tiptoe around struggle. But he does something far more valuable—he shows what it means to turn grit into generosity, to build bridges where walls could stand, and to leave a legacy measured not by trophies, but by lives touched.

You'll laugh at some of his stories. You might tear up. And I will tell you this: You will definitely find yourself inspired to do *more* with what you've already been given. And maybe, just maybe, you'll walk away ready to lift someone else, too.

That's the gift of knowing John Gullo.

And now, it's yours to share.

PART I
Roots & Finding My Wings

"Tomorrow is the most important thing in life. It comes to us at midnight, all clean and perfect and puts it in our hands, in hopes we learned something from yesterday."
– John Wayne

CHAPTER 1:

A Simple Start

"You are a product of your environment. So choose the environment that will best develop you toward your objective... Are the things around you helping you toward success— or are they holding you back?"
– W. Clement Stone

Ever seen the movie *Goodfellas*? Some of the early scenes take me directly back to my childhood. It could have been filmed in my very Italian neighborhood in Buffalo, New York, from the rundown tenement houses and apartment buildings to the swaths of wiseguys hanging around the streets. Buffalo's West Side was a two-lane morality play: family, church, and cannoli on one side; wiseguys, whispers, and quick money on the other. I didn't know it was unusual. It was just another Tuesday.

My family and I lived in an apartment above the grocery store, Ralabate's, on Busti Avenue. One half above the large grocery was a warehouse where we would play, and the other had been converted into apartments where an occasional rat swore squatters' rights. It was here that our family scratched out our existence. The competing grocery store in our neighborhood was Amato's, but Ralabate's was where my father worked as a meat cutter. That's about all I would know about him. Fortunately for me, I was surrounded by good food and the people who enjoyed it as much as I did.

I awoke each morning to the mouthwatering smell of homemade bread and other Italian pastries from the bakery down the block. As much as I loved to stuff myself with fresh-baked Italian bread, my favorite was cannoli: chocolate-covered and bursting with ricotta cream cheese. Just the smell had the power to make my stomach rumble. If you were a kid with an appetite and no money, it was both heaven and cruel torture.

By the time the sun rose, the street was already alive with contradiction. On the surface, lines were drawn in thick markers—good/bad, day/night, Italian/not. But life kept blurring the edges for me. It wasn't hard. Mafia influence wasn't whispered about in our neighborhood; it was the loud undercurrent. It was constant, humming, normal.

Soon enough, as I was growing, I would have to face the nuances of shadow between the dark and the light. You see, on the west side of Buffalo in the late '40s and especially the '50s, for young kids, our role models were those "wiseguys." These young men had flash, dash, and cash: slicked-back hair, expensive Italian suits, and beautiful, polished, state-of-the-art automobiles. Power wore cologne.

Our neighborhood literally buzzed with loud, frenetic energy. Everyone knew—or thought they knew—everyone else's business. Gossip moved from ear to mouth several times a day. You never knew what was true and what wasn't—but it sure made for an interesting life!

Across our street stood Scotties Bar, complete with an early version of a kiosk, an outdoor bar people could walk up to and order food. It was always busy, and by midmorning, the aroma of cooked crab slathered with butter, corn on the cob, and clams on the half shell wafted into my window and made my stomach growl louder. Scottie's was always crowded with old men who smoked like the railyard, drank at all hours, and told bawdy jokes I eagerly repeated to my friends. These old men kept a protective eye on the neighborhood—the entire Italian sector, really—and nothing got past them.

Mostly, they gathered around tables in small groups playing a game called *Morra*. An ancient form of gambling, this game dates back thousands of years to Greek and Roman times. It was all about "odds or evens," and it was fascinating for me to watch. Leaning a little dangerously out my window, I would carefully observe as each player held fingers behind his back, reflecting a secret number. When they brought them forward simultaneously, each called out their guesses as to the sum of all fingers revealed by all the players combined.

Winners roared their victories, and the losers? Well, you could say I learned to curse very colorfully at a young age.

Walking down my street, I heard all kinds of prismatic language thrown about, in half-English, half-Italian, like *"Ma tu sei pazzo!* You're crazy!" The most animated were the mothers, often scolding their large broods of children. "Don't you look at me like that, *faccia brutta*!" Then, their inevitable body language that spoke louder than words: SWAT! SWAT!

The gaggles of mothers and grandmothers intimidated me most. My friends and I were all third-generation Italian Americans. We were not taught Italian beyond "*mangiare, mangiare!*" for "eat, eat!" But those ladies would slip into Italian whenever they didn't want us kids to understand—which of course, made me listen harder. My first attempt at joining in, however, ended in disaster.

One afternoon, proud of my new vocabulary, I shouted, *"Buttanna! Buttanna!"* mimicking the old ladies as they gossiped—so pleased I'd picked up the full, vibrant pronunciation of this word. After all, these groups of women vehemently slung it about left and right as they gossiped about other women.

Next thing I knew, however, my body was wrenched over the kitchen sink, and my mouth was washed out with soap while I choked and cried. Only later did I find out the word I'd learned was a nuclear, ethnic word for "loose woman." The old ladies could yell it all day long… but for some reason, I wasn't supposed to say it—ever. So, I turned my attention toward other mischief.

On Busti Avenue, every afternoon after elementary school, the neighborhood kids and I enacted our revenge on the dreaded neighborhood rats who haunted us all in the night down dark alleys, and some inside our homes and apartments. It was *us vs. them*, and soon we found a game where, at times, we could come out on top.

On the second floor of the building, we opened the windows, where we could see the rats blatantly feeding on whatever they could get their paws on, scampering across the garbage lids in broad daylight. The nerve of them! We planned an attack like junior bombardiers.

"Ready—Aim—Fire!" yelled one of my friends.

"Bombs away!" I joined in.

"Give 'em the ol' Kenney Cocktail!" said another, referring to the famous M-47 bombings made by Gen. C. Kenney during WWII, just as we catapulted our makeshift bombs out the window. Using heavy metal marbles, or "aggies" as we called them, we didn't win the war… but we posted respectable numbers and learned to tell tall tales like the men on our street.

Once we grew tired of rat-bombing, we played Hide-and-Seek. I prided myself on being very good at being invisible. Twice, I hid so well that the sun went down and my friends went home. It's a special kind of victory when you play the game so well you scare your own mother half to death.

Another favorite was darts, though not the pub version, where we'd be shooed out of. Instead, we discovered that darts stuck beautifully into the wooden wall outside Ralabate's. From there, it escalated into a carnival sideshow: one kid stood against the wall, arms spread, while the others took target practice. It was exhilarating to throw. It was terrifying to be the target.

One afternoon, when it was my turn to be the carnival freak, I assumed "the position" while my trusted buddy threw next. Suddenly, I screamed bloody murder: "Get it out! GET IT OUT!" My buddy's thrown dart had lodged in the calf of my left leg. That ended my volunteer carnival career—fast.

Still, the streets were ours. We chased each other around corners until the music told us we'd strayed too far. Every ethnic neighborhood had its own radio station. If we heard polka or Irish ballads instead of Dean Martin or Louis Prima, we hightailed it back. Crossing into another territory after dark wasn't just risky—it could be dangerous. Our metropolitan area was very diverse, and I was quite fascinated. Alongside our Italian neighborhoods in Buffalo, there were Polish, Black, Irish, and Jewish sections—and none of them mixed after 5 p.m. Sure, fair commerce and polite friendliness existed during business hours, but at night, the ongoing battles for territory and control were real.

At home, my brother Jim and I never really got along as we were too far apart in age, and therefore, he saw me as a pest. He was hardly ever there. But I was a magical part of my sisters' world for a time. Rose, Joanne, Terri, and Jacque each got to play "mommy" with me as the baby and treated me like their favorite bendy doll. I was pampered and spoiled. Not with money, but with constant attention. I ate it up in gulps, like chocolate cannoli.

What I did know, even as a boy, was that my family was *poor*. I don't think I would have been as conscious of this if it were not for the fact that my siblings were acutely aware of this poverty. It was a part of their everyday conversations. Their craving for more shaped us all, but in different ways, like the scarcity mentality that seemed ingrained in our DNA.

For one thing, my father never owned a car. Mom didn't, either. We walked everywhere, during Buffalo's sizzling summers and blinding winters. If we were lucky, we might ride the bus for a nickel.

Then one day, my brother Jim, who was in high school, rolled up to the curb in his first automobile. Not your typical first teen car, either, like a beat-up Studebaker or Plymouth Belvedere. Jim pulled up in an Oldsmobile limousine, 98 Series Regency Brougham with seats for *nine* passengers. It felt like we'd been teleported.

Picking our jaws up off the sidewalk, my mother and sisters and I piled inside. Mom didn't dare ask Jim how he could afford this car as he took us on an outing to the rich section of town, where we gawked at the mansions. I would say we were speechless, but that never happened with the Gullo clan. Instead, the limo was filled with chatter. We oohed and ahhed over the next mansion as we had the last.

"Wouldn't it be great if we owned one of these?" my sisters asked dreamily.

Jim took us back to tour those neighborhoods time after time, and yet never in my wildest dreams did I think *I* might eventually own one. For one thing, it seemed too far-fetched, too pie-in-the-sky different from our reality. While my siblings obsessed over money, I cared more about people. What I didn't realize then was that I carried a deep wound: the desperate need to be accepted and wanted. My father was absent. My working mother was exhausted. My brother mostly ignored me, and my sisters' focus moved from me to boyfriends. All of this contributed to a yearning, an aching need inside of me that would shape my life for decades.

By the time I entered third grade, my mother was a single mom, and my father was completely out of the picture. I barely knew him beyond his white apron at the butcher counter anyway. No one talked about him. He and I never participated in a single activity together.

Jim? He hated the man outright. That he hated our father should have been enough for me, but I still wanted my dad—his attention, his love, *anything* that said he was somehow mindful of me.

One day in the third grade, Jim caught me crying from missing my ghost of a father—the man who had never really existed for me. In a huff, he drove me to our father's apartment, where he now lived separately from the rest of us. When we came to the door, my brother shoved me in, and just as quickly, my father threw me out.

"See?" Jim said scathingly. "That's the guy you wanted more of." And without another word, he took me home.

It wasn't until later that I learned my parents were forced together in a rather mafioso fashion.

My mother's birth name was Josephine, but everyone called her Rose. Her upbringing was rough. When she was just a baby, her 19-year-old mother became deathly ill from the Spanish Flu, which the CDC estimates infected over 500 million and killed over 50 million people worldwide in 1918.[1] Rose's father became anguished, watching his wife suffer and resigned to her death. After all, he was watching others drop like flies. Unable to bear the thought of watching her die, he took his own life behind a barn in Fredonia, New York, like some twisted version of Romeo and Juliet.

Miraculously, my grandmother survived long enough to marry Grandpa Orlando, whom my mother adored. When her mother died from illness just a few years later, instead of being raised with her kind stepfather, Orlando, my mother was given as a child to her Uncle Scanio because he was a "blood relative." Scanio, unfortunately, was borderline mafioso. I can say that because I was told by multiple sources that back in those days, he and his associates were experts at "squeezing" money out of unsuspecting people.

When my mother was just 13 years old, she was already beautiful. Uncle Scanio set her up on a "date" with Phillip, the man who would become our father.

Setting them up on a blind date sounds like a nice thing to do, doesn't it? It wasn't.

My dad, Phillip, who was ten years older than Rose, got to "spend the evening" with her. According to my mother, the very next day, Uncle Scanio accused Phillip of taking advantage of her. Only Scanio wasn't truly worried about my mother's honor in the least. Instead, he demanded hush money from Phillip's family, who then forced him to marry Rose.

Two young people, one still a child, both forced into marriage... neither ready, neither willing. No wonder it crumbled.

By the time I came along as the caboose, my mother had already given birth to six other children, all before turning twenty: Jim, Rose, Josephine (Joanne), Theresa (Terri), Jacqueline (Jacque), and another brother, Phillip, who died as a toddler.

---

1 "History of 1918 Flu Pandemic," Centers for Disease Control and Prevention, National Center for Immunization and Respiratory Diseases (NCIRD), https://archive.cdc.gov/#/details?url=https://www.cdc.gov/flu/pandemic-resources/1918-commemoration/1918-pandemic-history.htm.

As a kid, I didn't know any of these details. It was only as I got older that I realized my father's life was stolen from him by Uncle Scanio. *No wonder he didn't care about us*! We were a product of blackmail, not love.

My mother, toughened by tragedy, worked long hours at the factory of Merckens Chocolate Company. When she was home, she did her best to hold our family together. She may not have chosen the life she got, but she gave us all that she had, including attention, love, and kindness. After her divorce in 1950, we moved to Auburn Avenue into a large, three-story house that had been converted into five apartments: two on the first and second floor, and our family lived in the apartment on the third floor.

Our apartment had a rat infestation. They lived in the walls, and those rats were loud, especially at night. Always hungry, they constantly gnawed away at something as we tried to sleep. In the morning, we would kick the furniture to make sure none were under the bed or table. Survival, Buffalo-style. Still at night, I had a very real fear my toes would become a midnight snack.

In that apartment, we lived with my sister Terri and her husband, Daniel, who became my first real role model. Being the youngest in the family presented its own challenges—as well as its freedoms and blessings.

Amongst my new friends in the neighborhood, it seemed like everybody was called Tony or Joey. In fact, one good friend was Joey Ralabate. It was his father who owned Ralabate's grocery store and the meat market where my father worked. Another was Joey Aiello, the kid whose parents owned the bakery where the freshly baked bread and cannoli made my mouth water. I wished Mom would bake like that, but she always made sure there was food on the table. We never went hungry, and her motto was, "You may have holes in your pants, but they're always clean." She staked her pride on that.

Mom did her best to be a good example and carried that strong Italian sense of pride. Still, it was fun to poke at; I learned early how to push her buttons. When she sent us down to the railroad tracks to pick dandelions for salad and wild rhubarb to make desserts, I brought up the other creatures that visited the area.

"Mom, haven't these dandelions been watered by every passing dog?"

She shushed me, her face growing flushed. Suddenly, I noticed her washing the stems more vigorously. I loved to get her goat. But it didn't mean I could get away with everything.

I went shopping with my sisters once, and I stole a flashlight. I thought it was cool and hoped it would help keep the rats away from my toes! However, when I came home, the moment my mother saw me with something she knew I hadn't paid for, she marched me straight back to the store to confess what I'd done.

It was an important life lesson, one I took to heart, not only learning the price of a flashlight but the cost of losing your soul.

Even though I was left a lot to my own devices, Mom was super-strict with her teenage daughters—and for good reason. They were all beautiful Italian girls. Likely having to do with her own difficult upbringing, Mom wouldn't allow them to date. So, the girls developed a plan: they would leave the apartment together, promising Mom a group activity, but then secretly separate to do their own thing. When it was time to come home, they'd all meet to return together. Mom never had to be the wiser.

Once, however, the youngest sister, Jacque, did not get back on time. All of Buffalo heard about it when only three of the four girls returned. Mom's fury could shake a city block.

Mom wasn't exactly a perfect saint, either. One day, Mrs. Ralabate nearly beat down our door. *She could shake a city block herself*, I thought. My eyes were wide, but Mom wouldn't let her in, even as she called my mother every name in the book, echoing from outside our apartment, and down the stairs. Despite my extensive knowledge of Italian slang, I learned surprising new words and descriptive phrases—as her shrill voice shot out through every apartment in that house. I was embarrassed that this was my best friend, Joey Ralabate's mom. And from the way my mother's face was flushing,

I thought perhaps her accusation of Mom having an affair with Joey's father might have held some truth to it.

But who was I to judge? In our zero-lot-line house, I discovered I could make some cash with mirrors—and to me, it seemed harmless. The neighborhood boys paid a nickel or a dime for what they thought was their first burlesque show. In reality, the mirrors just reflected my sisters kissing their boyfriends in the living room when I set up the mirrors "just so." It was my first entrepreneurial venture. Looking back, it was certainly less innocent than a lemonade stand—but supply met demand, and I learned fast.

Life seemed grand! I took advantage of the fact that I was born in a leap year and had my sisters spoil me on my pretend birthday. But as each of my sisters dropped me like a hot lasagna to get married, suddenly I found myself mostly alone while Mom still worked long hours. I felt bereft.

Fortunately for me, my sister Terri and her husband still resided in our apartment with us. Terri stayed super busy taking care of her husband, Danny Paradowski, and learning computers, but I liked having a man around the house. Danny also worked long hours, and most often, I had no one to keep me out of trouble.

I became anxious and desperate to prove myself. That deeply held insecurity would lead to my biggest mistakes and yet also to my greatest successes. As Ted Turner would admit to once in an interview, I used the power of my anxiety and emotional insecurity to fuel and grow great things.[2] But first I had to learn how.

My buddies and I roamed the streets; I had no one to keep me out of trouble—and in Buffalo, it was in large supply.

---

2 "Ted Turner Looks Back," *CBS News*, November 7, 2008, https://www.cbsnews.com/news/ted-turner-looks-back/; https://achievement.org/achiever/ted-turner/.

Life Lessons

Despite segregation all around me in my early days, I never understood it. The choices people made based on other people's skin colors, religions, ethnicity, and backgrounds truly disturbed me. Maybe that's why I became the kind of person who made friends across the board with everyone. In my neighborhood, however, I learned quickly that you could love everybody—but you certainly couldn't trust them all. Not even family. But you still loved family and remained devoted to them. Mom taught me that you gave them your life's breath.

As a kid, I didn't realize how hard my mother truly had it until she finally revealed all the family secrets to me closer to the end of her life. I took her for a long car ride, where I asked the questions I had always wondered about. Then came the big question:

"So... did you ever love Dad?" This was one of the main questions that had plagued me for decades.

Mom sighed and looked out the window. "What do I know about love? I was playing with dolls and then having babies." She gave me a mischievous smirk while she admitted, "Your father was good in bed..." "Aha!" I exclaimed. "That explains seven kids in the family." Until she added, "...but he really did not want me." She went on to tell me he didn't see her as a person; she was just someone he owned.

Society's rules were different then, which is why she stayed with him for so long. Divorce was frowned upon, especially in our Catholic community. I was happy that she had found so much joy in her second, real love. Later, when she was dying, she couldn't shake her Italian Catholic roots and still thought she was going to hell because of her divorce.

It took me a lifetime to heal my childhood wounds and religious beliefs, so I was in no place to judge her.

And this I know: Mom was a great woman, and I will see her somewhere brighter.

CHAPTER 2:

Veni, Vidi, Vici

"I came, I saw, I conquered."
– Julius Caesar

"Adversity is the diamond dust that heaven polishes its jewels with."
– Thomas Carlyle

On the Italian streets of Buffalo, if power wore cologne, most of the young men grabbed a whiff. My brother Jim? He stole the bottle.

Mom didn't want me to turn out like my older brother, who was starting to resemble Uncle Scanio; he was erring on the side of mafioso, at least where girls, money, and power were concerned. Even though Jim largely ignored me, I was still curious about him. In our neighborhood, he was considered one of the cool kids. Jim, a big man-on-campus senior, drove around in his limo like he was a god himself. He'd pick up a whole pack of girls from school, drop off the ones he wasn't interested in, and bring his favorite back to our garage. Shuttle service with fringe benefits. My brother parked his Oldsmobile in the garage when he came home from school or work and never came into the house.

One day, I got nosy and peeked inside, trying to eavesdrop. There was a girl in there with him, and they were making out. I didn't bother trying to skim a nickel or dime off that show. While my sisters would have smacked me had they caught me, still, they would have forgiven me. Jim, I had no doubt, would have killed me.

When I got older, he smugly let me in on a brazen secret: he was a driver for a meat packing company, and every so often, an "extra" beef carcass would fall off the truck, so to speak. Between deliveries, he sold sides of beef to markets not on his route. The inside guys got their cut, and Jim pocketed the rest. When *The Irishman* hit theaters in 2019, I didn't analyze the cinematography. I exclaimed, "Holy shit—that's Jim!"

Jim developed a receding hairline early, which made him seem older than the rest of his friends. His next car was a '48 Buick convertible with a zebra-skin interior that turned heads, especially among his mafia friends. On days he took our mother for a ride, people thought they were boyfriend and girlfriend. Despite being in her early forties, she still turned heads—she was that stunning.

Most people don't realize that "mafia" comes from the Sicilian *mafioso*, meaning swagger, bravado, boldness.[3] That was Jim to a tee. But the wiseguys in our neighborhood weren't just about being ostentatious. They were becoming dangerous. Mafia life was shifting from swagger to authority, laced with bringing fear, from respect to absolute control.

This is why Catholic school was foisted upon me. My mother's hope was that I would have better influences there than on the streets.

At elementary school, church came before class every morning. I was proud to be an altar boy—it was what every Catholic boy wanted. Once, when Bishop Burk of the Buffalo Diocese led Christmas Mass, about twenty of us altar boys knelt through an hour of incense, candles, prayers, and Communion. Afterward, as he passed us, he said, "You boys have been kneeling long enough. Get up!"

---

3 "mafioso," *Merriam-Webster.com*, n.d., https://www.merriam-webster.com/dictionary/mafioso

Best homily ever.

Not long after that, I learned my first English four-letter word from Father Monroe. One day, when I was opening the large doors to the cathedral, a gust of wind caught the door and slammed it shut with a *BANG!*

Startled, Father Monroe exclaimed, "Hell's bells!" The class was shocked, and I quietly filed that one away with my growing vocabulary of irreverence.

I actually thought I wanted to be a priest. I was very shy, for one thing. There was even a time when I would practice saying Mass at a pretend altar I built from boxes in our basement. Then I learned about girls, and celibacy was not in my future. Neither, I guess, was reverence.

Case in point: Sister Beatrice. If she caught us out of line, she'd bark, "Hands on the desk!" then whack our fingers with her pointer. My hands stung for days. I learned quickly to avoid her radar—but I seemed naturally inclined to shenanigans.

One day, I was kept after school in detention with a bunch of kids because we were misbehaving while walking from one class to another. Father Monroe came in through the door as we were headed down the stairs towards the detention hall.

"Sister," he said gravely, "what do we have here?"

I called out, "Ma Barker's Killer Brood!" referencing a notorious gangster family that a movie had been named after. Father Monroe didn't laugh. He slapped me with an extra hour of detention.

That detention I absolutely deserved. Corporal punishment? Maybe. But the psychological torment I would come to witness for myself… that I would never forget.

My sister Joanne was the first to marry outside the Catholic Church. When she and her fiancé Gene met with the priest, he told them they couldn't marry in the church because Gene wasn't Catholic—unless they paid a "special fee." That bribe bought them the altar and a proper Mass. I was outraged—so much for holiness.

This was my introduction to plenary indulgences—the Church's tradition of paying off punishment for sin. It's why Martin Luther had left the Church over this centuries earlier.[4] Meanwhile, the mafia guys in our neighborhood went to confession religiously and filled the Sunday basket, confident their donations kept their souls in good standing, since a Catholic sinner could pay money to enter back into "a state of grace" and get into heaven when they died.

Once my sisters were gone, I couldn't count on making money from peep shows, so I had to get serious. Mom was too poor to offer an allowance, so I had to find other entrepreneurial endeavors. One winter day after school, I was hanging out with friends in the neighborhood when we "accidentally" discovered that a house had been left unlocked. All of us snuck in, thinking it was the world's greatest game. There, we found over $100 in dollar-saving coupons. I took them and used them, figuring I wouldn't lose my soul, as they should have locked their doors.

I helped our landlord clean out the basement of trash, and I became responsible for killing rats. Mom was a cleaning fanatic, so she taught me how to clean properly. She also taught me about the ability to trust an eating establishment—or not. "If the windows are dirty," she said with disgust, "don't trust it. The rest will be dirty." I never forgot that, and the lesson served me later in life.

Shortly after that, when I was ten and in the fifth grade, it was decided that Mom and Terri and Danny and I would move to Kenmore, New York, together. It felt like such a big change to leave all my current friends to make new ones. Now we shared a duplex with a Polish family, and Mom got a new job at a factory building pianos. When she came home, slumped over and wincing, I could tell it was wrecking her back. The worst part was, Danny went into the service and was shipped out to Germany for two years, and that's when everything changed.

Fatherless and rudderless for two years, I got involved with guys from the neighborhood. I always looked older than I was, so despite being in elementary school, I often hung out with high school guys.

---

4 Encyclopedia Britannica: "Originally intended to promote academic discussion, Luther's theses became a manifesto that turned a protest about a German indulgence scandal into the greatest crisis in the history of Western Christianity."

Many of them experimented with bad stuff. Coming from latchkey backgrounds, like me, we were *all* unsupervised and wild.

One of our main games was to jump in a car with vinyl seats in the summer, shut all the windows until it got furnace-hot, just to see who would have to get out first and who could handle the heat of staying in. It was a test of courage—and stupidity.

One spring day before I graduated from elementary school, my buddies and I "borrowed" a car. None of the guys was a licensed driver. As we lurched around the city, I suddenly understood why it was called a "joyride." It became a trend with us until one afternoon, when we heard the sirens and saw the flashing light. While the rest of us hung on for dear life, the driver sped away. The moment our buddy slammed to a stop, we all bolted out of the car in multiple directions and hid. By the time the officer caught up with the car, we were nowhere to be seen. The run-in with the police should have stopped us, but getting away only fueled future antics.

I was rapidly losing my innocence, and like my siblings, I found myself in need of money. I picked up part-time work at a collision shop. My "job" was providing "replacement" car parts. Customers paid for repairs, my buddies and I got the thrill of a small heist, and I learned the basics of bodywork. No paycheck, just adrenaline and a front-row seat in the shop.

Kenmore, though close, wasn't mafia territory like Buffalo. Still the mischief was just as real. One late spring day at school, some of the guys thought it would be hilarious to shatter ink bottles against the walls of the school. We laughed as the ink splattered across the bricks. Unfortunately, I was the one who got caught red-handed; my punishment was cleaning off all the bricks—and it was not easy!

Fortunately, my brother-in-law Danny finally came home from the military. I knew he and my sister Terri were having problems, but I was too young to understand. I just knew he was a hard-working guy who, in my mind, could figure out the solution to anything. I straightened up a lot when he was around, and I did almost everything he asked. A child of divorce, I craved the father-son relationship, and Danny provided that for me. His expectations were big, and I loved meeting them. For one thing, our house was heated by coal. That fall and winter, my job was to go downstairs first thing in the morning and shovel the coal into the furnace. It taught me discipline and gave structure to my days.

Danny, an amateur photographer, took family photos, pictures of dogs and scenery, and photos of a different nature. One day, when I was by myself, I was curiously exploring his dark room. That's when I discovered he was also taking indiscretionary pictures of his wife. I absconded with some photos of my sister, and when Danny found out, he beat the living crap out of me.

Strangely, I didn't get mad at him for it. I learned from his discipline instead. He began to mold me into the man I would one day become. A profound realization? Being bad taught me what being good should look like.

My brother-in-law seemed to sense I was at a crossroads and actively tried to find more positive outlets. He'd begun working for a drum manufacturing business called Drummer's Paradise, and I was astonished one day when he brought me home my first snare drum. Along with the landlord's son, Teddy Dworakowski, we started playing just for fun. Both of us actually got pretty good, and we would have "drum wars" to see who could keep in rhythm longer with drum rolls and beats.

After that, Danny made me my first set of drums and cymbals. They were gorgeous, awesome-sounding drums! Black with gold hairs, they had mother-of-pearl spread throughout them. For a kid with nothing, this was *everything*. To have someone who believed in me was life-changing. I would give this drumming all I had. And, to the chagrin of my mother and neighbors, I learned how to play that full set of drums in the basement of our house... every single day.

Benny Goodman's "Sing, Sing, Sing" became my anthem. I learned Gene Krupa's drum solo by ear, listening to a cheap Westinghouse turntable. Written notes and math baffled me, but if I heard it once, I could play it. Drums became my magic, pulling me out of mischief. After school, it absolutely became *the* fun thing to do, rather than stealing cars or car parts. It was as if Danny knew it would be the magic that truly changed me from the ruffian kid into a better version of myself—although it didn't make me an angel. Just less of a hellion.

Danny also taught me baseball. As a great athlete himself, he taught me persistence. When I got into high school, I went out for the Cardinal Dougherty High School football team. To my dismay, my name wasn't listed on the roster. Doggedly determined, I found my own pads, trained harder, and kept showing up. Eventually, I earned a spot—and a letterman jacket.

That experience taught me that if I wanted something badly enough, I had to fight for it. And when I fought for it, I could get it. That also kept me out of *some* trouble. Still, pranks always seemed to find me.

Our high school was brand new. In our first year, it served only freshmen. Built in a rather swampy area of Buffalo, the grounds were covered in frogs—to the point you had to watch your step. One day, my buddy and I captured a bunch. Eyes wide with fright in anticipation of getting caught, we snuck into the Latin teacher's room during lunch. The teacher was Father Leger, who had an innocent nature about him. This made him our target.

After lunch, back in the classroom, he wondered why we were all there *before* the bell. *Carpe Diem* wasn't exactly our schtick, as we generally slammed into our seats at the last minute.

Then the poor priest opened his briefcase.

Frogs exploded from the opening, leaping out in multiple directions. Chaos and pandemonium followed; it was an eerie reminder of my joyriding days—a little too much on the edge. We were never fingered, but our whole class was in trouble. Fortunately, no one seemed to mind. The look on Father Leger's face had been priceless and became the stuff of school legend.

Despite being shy, especially around girls, I had a lot of fun. I couldn't help my sense of humor, and my mouth often got me into trouble. My teachers usually interrupted my comic routine with, "Gullo, shut it."

One day, a kid in one of my classes, Thomas Dunn, was hanging around with some others while I was cutting up before the last class of the day.

The teacher raised an eyebrow and asked, "Are you done?"

"Oh no, I'm not Dunn," I said with a straight face. "He's in the other third row. I'm Gullo." That brought on gales of laughter from the crowd... and a glare from the teacher. *Ribbit.*

Despite my attendance at Catholic school, my mother continued to be scared for me. My brother was still living a fast life and had gotten his girlfriend, Carole, pregnant. They'd had to get married, and I'd become a young uncle.

That year, my mom met James F. Robinette. He was the fire captain of his department. Everyone called him "Red," even though his head was graying quite a bit and he'd lost most of his red-colored hair. As he and Mom began dating, I found I admired him immediately. I mean, he was a firefighter! I thought that was cool—and rather heroic. I especially liked the way he treated every person on his fire crew, regardless of race or religion, with the same respect... as long as they earned it.

Mom and Red married when I was fifteen, and I couldn't have been happier for her. We moved again, this time to Niagara Falls. It was tough to upend schools again, but fortunately, Terri and Danny bought a house across the street. I was relieved. I loved them with all my heart and wanted to stay close to them.

At this age in Niagara Falls, I also needed money. I figured, with the fresh start and Danny and Red around, I wanted to do it legitimately. I got my first real—meaning *legal*—job as a clown. Dressed in a garishly bright costume, my hair big and fluffy, my face painted and topped with a red nose, I waved a flag to capture the attention of passersby to the brand-new Hess gas station. I worked after school during daylight hours and in the summer, sometimes up to three hours a day. I was motivated. I had to count on myself for the cash I needed.

My love for playing the drums stayed constant. Rain or shine, I practiced daily. Neighbors hated it. Mom hated it. Red tolerated it.

But the drums gave me friends and started opening doors when I started meeting other kids who loved music and establishing new and important friendships.

Then out of the blue, my biggest rock, my role model, my compass, hit too low of a low to come out of. Danny pulled over at a park in Tonawanda and climbed a tree where he hung himself. I was a senior at my high school when they called me to identify his body, because they didn't want to disturb his wife. That image burned into me forever.

It was at that funeral, through snatches of whispers and eavesdropping on conversations of the piles of food around the table, that I learned the complexity of the troubles facing my brother-in-law. Danny had shared with me that his father was a drunk. He'd left Danny to raise his siblings. An affair while serving in Germany added charged tension in his marriage as he and Terri tried to work things out after his return home. Shorter and slender, Danny struggled with an inferiority complex. While he'd excelled as an MP in the military, when he got home, he couldn't seem to make anything work for long. He fought his demons his whole life—until it got to be too much.

I felt like a hole had been torn open in my chest. This worsened when I learned that the Catholic church would not give him the sacrament of the last rites. Father Monroe, the priest I knew from St. Joseph's, had transferred to Niagara Falls. I went straight to him to request Danny's last rites, but he also refused since Danny had taken his own life.

"Listen," I said, barely able to keep the tears out of my voice. "Listen, I climbed up that tree. You can't tell me that he was in his right mind and that God is sending him to hell!" The Church and Father Monroe didn't agree. Terri was devastated. I was shattered.

As the days and weeks passed, somehow life didn't crush me. The distinct loss of Danny made me lean on my new role model, Red. In the first year of their marriage, Mom and Red fought often. When Mom threatened to leave Red during these newlywed disagreements, I finally told her, "No. I'm staying. Solve it. I'm happy here." That stunned her—and we stayed. If it were not for that, I probably would have lost my way. Red didn't have children from any previous relationships, so I was the first kid he raised. He took it seriously.

Mom hoped Catholic school would save me, but it was actually two men in my life who started me on the more straight and narrow path. Because of Danny and Red, I was getting set in school, making new friends, learning to find my own compass, and bonding with my new stepfather instead of fighting against him. Even though I'd lost Danny, I finally had a solid and stable man in my life, and for the first time, I wasn't visiting trouble... at least not every day.

Red became "Dad." Not by blood, but by choice.

And sometimes, that's thicker.

Life Lessons

I tell my grandkids now, "You learn more what not to do in life than you do what to do." Like my brother, my earlier days were influenced by the wiseguys in the area. Unfortunately for him, it colored his business and relationships for the rest of his life. Fortunately for me, I learned a lot of what not to do… and would find guidance from significant people on what *to* do in my formative years. I also had a different sort of innocence and naivety that served me.

I longed to find that same type of guidance and anchor inside my church, but I learned the hard way that the Catholic Church had its flaws. Religion seemed built around guilt and fear. Plus, how was it that doing anything fun meant we were damned?

The church went so far as to teach that a person must get baptized because of original sin, but I never understood that concept. If Jesus died for our sins already, then how could we have sins *at birth,* 2000 years later?

I also decided not to get hung up on scripture the way most people did and began to step away from dogma… praying to the God and Jesus I knew, not to rituals I couldn't trust.

Later, I'd learn different doctrines from different faiths, but one truth stuck: Jesus taught kindness and love. And that's what mattered.

I also held tight to one belief that gave me tremendous hope: I would see Danny again one day. Booker T. Washington said, "There are two ways of exerting one's strength; one is pushing down, the other is pulling up." Because of Danny and Red, for the rest of my life, I want to be the kind of person that pulls other people up.

CHAPTER 3:

True Father, True Mentor

"The heart of a father is the masterpiece of nature."
– Prevost Abbe

I started out in life as a follower, not a leader. Even in high school, I wanted so badly to be accepted that I experimented with the same things my friends did—just because they were doing them. Although I was sheltered in many ways at home, I had no one consistently teaching me the right way to do things. Sure, Danny had disciplined me when he came home from the service—but he had never really talked things out or mentored me.

Living with Red, however, was a very different experience.

My stepfather turned out to be a great mechanic and a great cook... though I never learned either skill from him. (Later I'd joke that my son Johnny was the son Red always wanted: king of the kitchen, grill, and demolition derby.)

To the outside world, Red was unassuming, yet he let me see the greater man inside—and he was full of dichotomies. For example, despite having never graduated from grade school, he was one of the wisest men I'd ever known. He was an agnostic, yet also the best

Christian I ever met. He knew the Bible inside out. He just didn't buy into organized religion.

That first winter after moving to Niagara Falls, I went ice skating. I carefully put the brand-new shoes I'd earned into the cubby. When I returned from the ice, however, I discovered that my precious shoes were stolen. I couldn't believe it! Plus, I had to walk home in my skates, and by the time I got there, my ankles were so sore, I could hardly walk.

The crazy thing was, the very next day at school, I walked into class, and there were my shoes—on another kid's feet! I knew because they were brand new, with one particular scuff mark. Furious, I confronted my classmate. He denied it and walked home, still wearing my shoes.

I went home and told Red, who listened to my every word. Getting involved, he helped me get them back. That's when Red sat me down in the living room and introduced me to *his* version of the Golden Rule:

"John," he said seriously, "Don't shit on nobody… and don't let nobody shit on you."

I looked at him wide-eyed. He added, "If that don't get you into heaven, maybe it's not worth going!"

Before Red married my mom, he had the first MG Coupe on the East Coast. It was a sports car, a hip roadster. Now that he was a married man, he got rid of it. Being the cool guy he was, however, he replaced his Coupe with a sleek, black Austin-Healey. It had two little jump seats in the back just for me. He told me it was his "family" car, which made me laugh. I loved running around town in something so beautiful, knowing that Red had bought it with me in mind.

As Red and Mom settled into their marriage, peace began to grow in our home. Red took the time to explain life to me as we went. No one had ever done that before. And little by little, he became my north star, so I could learn how to find my own way in the world and not get lost. That was good, because there were a lot of competing voices in the world about right and wrong.

One night, Red and Mom took me to Jim's house in a suburb of Buffalo, called Wellsville. They were going out to dinner with my brother and his wife, and I was stuck watching Jim's kids. Red parked his Healey in front of the 24-foot cabin cruiser in the driveway. The boat was stabilized on pontoon supports.

As soon as the adults left, I called my friends. "Party time!"

That's the night I received the biggest lesson of my life. It changed me forever.

When the party was really going, it was time to show off. I went out to the car, started the purring motor, and revved the engine. It sounded so cool!

I'm going to be getting my license in the next year, after all, I justified it to myself. *I can handle this—and the girls will love it!*

Everyone surrounded the car to look at it, and I tried to back it up for my audience. Thinking I had put the car in reverse, when I revved the engine again and popped the clutch, it dropped into 2nd gear. The car shot forward, and I drove that beautiful Austin-Healey right under Jim's boat, where it remained, wedged tight.

Boy, you should see how fast my friends scattered! They were not even that fast when the cops were after them.

Red and Jim and their wives came home. Red was quite... inebriated. I told him what I'd done, but he said nothing and went to bed. I couldn't sleep and sat in dread that next morning. Only Red didn't talk to me about that next day, or the day after, or the day after that. Guilt stuck to my ribs like barbecue sauce. I was wading in it.

Two weeks later, I thought maybe I was going to get away with my stupidity when Red sat me down on the back porch.

"You realize what you've done?" I hung my head. He didn't even need to tell me what he was referring to.

"Yeah," I said, unable to meet his eyes, drowning in my shame. "I started the car without permission and then drove it under the boat and smashed it up."

"No," he said, and I looked up into his eyes, surprised. "No, son, you've lost my trust. You have to understand what that means. When you were born, you got a name. It was a good name, but it's what you *do* with that name that's important. Now that you've lost my trust, you need to earn back your good name."

"What are you going to do to punish me?" I asked timidly. After all, all forms of torture resembling the Spanish Inquisition had been running through my imagination for two weeks.

"Punish yourself," he said, and got up and walked into the house, shutting the door behind him. I was astounded.

That talk landed harder than any punishment—the fact that respect means more than even love. You can love someone but not respect them, blood or not. I wanted to regain Red's respect, even more than his love.

Without having to be pressed, in minutes, I knew exactly what I would have to do. Immediately, I set about getting another job and earned enough money to fix Red's car—which would take a long, long time. I also really did punish myself. I declared that I would not apply for my driver's license until I was 18, and I knew I would keep my word.

In my junior year, redistricting took place, and my classmates and I moved to LaSalle Public High School, where we were all forced into a scholarship curriculum that was over my head. Between my lousy grades and living just above the poverty line—even with Red's help—I knew I was not destined for college.

I should have been taking business courses, but instead, during school, I continued to be the class cut-up and was always in trouble with the teachers. One day, my Geometry teacher looked out the window and commented on the beauty of the dandelions in the school yard. I jumped out of the window, picked her a bouquet, and brought them to her.

"Principal's office!" she ordered.

By next week, she gave me a library pass. She said it was so I'd study, but we both knew it was just to get me completely out of her class so I wouldn't disrupt it. I took her up on that library pass so often that I failed the class and had to repeat it. But I got out of it what I wanted and thought I needed. Despite being shy, now everyone in school knew who I was.

It was with another teacher, Mrs. Parone, in American History, where I found my stride. This teacher actually enjoyed debate, and I enjoyed having a teacher who believed in frank and open discussion. We framed arguments often, and one about Harry Truman I found particularly fun. In studying Truman, it seemed to me from my school textbooks and in my young mind that he felt the United States had a moral and strategic obligation to support "free peoples" resisting subjugation by totalitarian regimes. I argued against giving aid to Greece and Turkey—that we needed to take care of our own. A very lively exchange erupted between Mrs. Parone and me, and we got the whole class involved. I decided I liked being an instigator when it was appreciated.

To my surprise, instead of taking a study hall for the second half of the school year, Mrs. Parone asked me to take her course again. Not because I failed, but as she explained, "Your debating enhances my curriculum." I glowed. That was a high compliment, especially coming from her. Of course, I retook the course and loved the challenge of it all.

Meanwhile, I practiced drums constantly. Red was a strict disciplinarian, and when I was mad at him or the chores he poured on me, I'd pound out "Running Bear, Little White Dove" with extra boom-boom fury. Passive aggression, percussion-style.

I fell in with some Polish neighborhood musicians: sax, guitar, piano. Together, we formed a band with the moniker "Lucky and His Sons of Vitches." At the same time, I teamed up with Mark Quackenbush, sax player, and Joey Casale, piano player, and we formed a jazz trio, known as "The Sundowners." I loved jazz! It was the best for a percussionist.

Even better was when Joey Casale's dad, who owned a bar and restaurant, invited us to play for his customers. A couple more guys came along as rock and roll was just getting hot. So we formed a rock band called "Hermie and the Spermies."

Mom hated our band names. Funny thing, the crowds didn't.

We started playing in bars on the weekends. In our rock 'n' roll band, our signature song was "The Peppermint Twist," made popular by Joey D and the Starlighters. I was having fun, making a few bucks, and grateful for the food and free drinks. The legal drinking age in New York was 18 in 1960. I'd always looked older than my age, and now with the help of football, I was a beefcake that people took for 19 or 20.

I loved being part of three different bands with three unique sounds. But it was the girls who were the best part. They seemed to easily develop crushes on nerdy band members. It was fun to see them mesmerized by all the guys on stage—even me. It disarmed me but secretly delighted me when married women hit on me!

However, after hearing some rumors, innuendos, and some of my stories (about girls, not booze), Red sat me down in their living room. Mom was sitting on the opposite side of the little room in a chair facing us.

Straight-faced, Red said, "John, I'm your father. Now tell me how you handle yourself when you're with a girl, and maybe I can give you a few pointers."

I was shocked. My face turned pink. I couldn't help but notice in the midst of my embarrassment, Mom's ears perked up. Perhaps for the first time in my life, I did not know what to say.

"John, listen to me," Red repeated as he leaned in, "when you take a girl for a ride, pull over somewhere quiet. Kiss her soft, not hard."

I stared, frozen, my mouth open. Mom's eyes were even wider than mine.

"Then," Red continued, "you take her hand and put it in your pants. If she blushes or pulls away, take her home and don't waste your night."

My mouth still wide open, I could only nod... and maybe blink.

I looked over at Mom, equally shocked, but when I looked back at Red, he was trying hard not to lose it from laughing so hard. At Mom's face, he let out a mighty chuckle, and we all laughed for a hot minute. Then all of a sudden, Red became completely serious again.

"Now, John, listen. Hormones are real. When you have a beautiful girl in your arms, human instincts are going to make you want to do something you shouldn't do. So, here's the deal: if that situation arises, you look her right in her eyes and ask yourself, *Can I be married to her for the rest of my life?* Because damn it, if you go any further, you'd better have already made that decision."

Now that was the start of great wisdom from a real father. My biological father never deserved the label. Red always deserved it: Dad. Father. Mentor.

At home, Red taught me more than how to respect women. He taught me how to fix things, paint, and clean—and use machinery the right way. His house had aluminum siding, and every spring I would literally wash the house from top to bottom. In Niagara Falls, when it snowed, he had a monster of a handheld snowplow, and I got permission from him to use it, as long as I was careful. During the week, I was allowed to make extra money for myself, doing other people's driveways when ours was done. I was still working hard to pay off the Healey and the boat, so I took every single job I could. Playing in the bars was the most lucrative.

With Red's sex education always in the back of my mind, it slowed me down. Truly, it kept me out of a lot of trouble. I did the dating thing for two years, and during that time, I never forgot those lessons, even when my rock band got a gig at a bar on Falls Street, right at the first street coming off the bridge from Canada. The drinking age in Canada was 21, so you guessed it—pretty Canadian girls flocked over to the States on weekends.

To get the crowd riled up, I worked the drums and the mic. When beautiful girls were out dancing in front of us, I would say, "Oh yeah, baby, we love it; do it to us all night long." My signature schtick: when two women walked in, I'd drum roll, stop the band, and announce, "Ladies and gentlemen, Sally Tucker and her mother... *Mother Tucker!*" The crowd howled, even if those two might not have. I also changed the words to Ray Charles' "What I Say." The new lyrics were risqué. Crowds loved that, too.

Playing the drums camouflaged my introverted personality. I wasn't John Gullo, I was the entertainer—and could practice charm while I was taking a break from the set. It got me out of my shell.

My final spring of high school, I squeaked out a C– average—but I *did* graduate! I soon realized it was time to think more like a grown-up in terms of who I was going to be and what I would do for work for the rest of my life. I got a job as a cleanup guy in Valinti's Meat Market. It was in North Tonawanda, and without a car, there was no mass transportation that could get me anywhere close.

Hitchhiking to work was risky. Once, a man offered me a ride. Soon, his conversation became suggestive. At a red light, I bailed. Nothing against him, but I knew exactly who I was—and it wasn't that.

Due to that experience, I knew I had to quit, so I switched to Federal Meat Market in Niagara Falls. My job was primarily cleanup, but at times, they let me debone brisket bones for trim to make hamburger and break out the kidney from the suet. I was learning a lot and felt like I was becoming a meat cutter! My birth father had been a meat cutter, but it was a simple coincidence that I was here. I wasn't following in his footsteps (because, frankly, I never liked where his led). But my beginnings in the field meant a good job and the ability to move up.

When management tossed perfectly good bones to save labor costs, I was crushed. But it was my first real lesson in economics: time management and cost vs. income.

I still struggled with insecurity, so I needed to be the best—and I hated being told no. I was burning to move up. One meat cutter told me, "You don't become a meat cutter that fast!" Funny thing is, years later, I became his boss!

When I celebrated my 18th birthday, Red said, "Son, you're old enough to drink now. Come on; let's go out."

Never in a million years would I admit this would *not* be my first drink, and off we went to Duggars Bar, where he got me intoxicated. Okay, we got drunk. Very, very, very drunk. In fact, we ended up in front of our house, sitting on the curb, puking our guts out.

The next day, my head throbbing, Red sat me down.

"See? Ain't that fun?"

So, the good news was that I remembered how horrible getting violently sick was—and didn't really want to feel that way, ever again. After that, I primarily stayed sober.

The week after my 18th birthday, Red began charging me rent. My friends thought my stepfather was cruel. I thought he was wise. Budgeting came with lessons: life insurance and saving for the future. He made me imagine the children I didn't have yet—and what I wanted for them. So, once I had enough for rent, he taught me how to budget the rest.

Red even made me buy a life insurance policy. At first, I thought he was nuts until he said, "In twenty years, you can cash it in to send your son or daughter to college." I never would have learned any of that on my own! It was compelling to me. I didn't even have a wife or kids yet, but a driving force inside of me was to give them a much better life than I'd experienced.

Finally, after years of work, I paid off the Healey and the boat. Fair punishment.

"Now, can you teach me to drive?" I asked, expecting Red to take me that weekend to learn.

"That's great!" he exclaimed. Then he grinned. "Buy a car for yourself, and when you have your own and your own insurance, I'll teach you how to drive my car—just ask."

Wow. Another lesson delivered.

Red taught me another "commandment" that stuck with me throughout my life, and the endeavors I would be involved in:

"Everything cometh to he who waiteth—as long as he worketh like helleth while he waiteth."

Life Lessons

I never forgot any of Red's lessons, and I put them to use! I also share them often with others.

When I was still enraged with the Catholic church over Danny, I discovered my new father was a reader and spiritual in his own way. "You don't need brick and mortar to believe in God," he said. He continued, "Every church is going to have faulty representatives because we're *human*. Even then, you've got to learn to find your own intuition about right and wrong."

I learned a lot about right and wrong just by watching how Red handled life and leadership. As a career firefighter, he served thirty years and retired as Battalion Chief in charge of apparatus. Once, I was hanging out at the firehouse with him and his crew when a guy running for NF City Council strode cockily into the fire hall to solicit the firefighters' support for his campaign. Everyone, especially the politician, gaped when my father grabbed him by the seat of his pants and threw him out the door. "Get away with your political bullshit! Stop pretending. You've already proven you don't care about us!"

That was Red. Honest. Direct. Fearless.

And he taught, "Be honest. If you make a mistake, just clean it up." My dad lived that. He would tell me he was sorry if he messed up or yelled at me for something I did not do. He came clean, and I learned that it wasn't humiliating to communicate faults; it was humility. And in that humility was living leadership that brought people together.

Simple Communication Math

Since watching Red, I've noticed through the years how people too often have problems with miscommunication. In my own example, I used to write in all caps when I was typing texts and emails because it was easier and less likely I would mess something up. Later, someone told me that meant I was "yelling." Well, of course,

I quit using all caps, but now our phones are always messing up texts for us!

Believe me, when you need to get something important across, take the time to make a phone call.

In life, I learned that everything is addition and subtraction. Figure out how you can add to someone's life, not take away from it. Simple. But if you try to keep score, to multiply and divide, you complicate everything! In relationships, use the KISS system: "Keep It Simple, Stupid." That is always the best approach.

Unforgettable

I would never forget Red's sex education course in my front room, with my mother present. Decades later, I would tell that story when I was teaching young men and women at church about chastity, hoping they'd ask themselves that question: *Could you spend the rest of your life with this person?* I was deeply involved with kids and teens in Ogden City, and I'd been chagrined to learn from the director of the Children's Justice Center that there were approximately 900 active cases of child abuse. I would share Red's crazy birds and bees talk and then end my own version of my pep talk with my own straight-shooting: "When a couple is not ready to commit to one another and a child is born, that child might suffer—your child, *your* baby that you brought into the world. Don't do it. Withhold that moment; wait until you're with the right person at the right time. I promise; it's worth it."

Red taught me to judge people by how they treated the waitress, the neighbor, the stranger on the street. He taught me simplicity: add where you can, subtract what you must—but don't multiply drama or divide people. He taught me survival, what to thrive really meant, and how to take responsibility, not just for my life, but for others.

On my own through the years, I learned from him to take the time to find out what people stand for and believe in, to form relationships on common ground. Even when I want to, I don't throw them out on their ass. It probably helped that I'd heard since I was a kid, "Judge not, lest ye be judged."

Many decades later, my friend's daughter came out to Mexico to stay for a bit. She was far left liberal and started to argue with me on all kinds of issues. "Hold on a second," I said, "let me put this on the table. I don't care what your religion is, the color of your skin, or what your politics are. What I care about is how you treat me and what you should care about is how I treat you."

From there we became fast friends.

Most of all, Red drilled this into me:

Love can fade, but respect endures.

And respect, once earned, makes love that much richer.

CHAPTER 4:

First Love, New Life

"Life is either a daring adventure or nothing at all."
– Helen Keller

On the weekends in the bars, dating mostly older women as a drummer, I enjoyed the hell out of it, learning how to "show up."

Still, I knew drumming wasn't a lasting career. We certainly weren't The Beatles.

Eventually I wanted to find a girl, settle down, have a white picket fence and a family, but one step at a time. A year out of high school without a decent job, I took the first step to enlist in the Army. In the interim, I got a job in Buffalo, New York, my old stompin' grounds. This position was at Bygall's Meat Market. They believed in me and took me on as an apprentice cutter. I was thrilled. My military career? It never got off the ground.

When I was nineteen and working a gig at a bar on the weekend, I met a fabulous woman named Christine. She was beautiful and smart. She had her own career as a nurse, and that impressed me. From the start, I was smitten. She, however, wasn't impressed. She was always trying to set me up with her friends—for good reason. Christine was four years older, from a staunch Polish family named

Pietkiewicz (though they went by Peters). They were Polish through and through, and I was a young, punk Italian kid. I wasn't exactly their idea of dating material.

But finally, she noticed me on the dance floor. Christine was an exceptional dancer, and I wasn't half bad myself after years of weekend practice. I learned I could dodge bar fights by dancing. I could also impress girls by making *them* look good on the dance floor.

My best pickup line was simple:

"You're really cute, and I know you've heard a lot of lines. So, let's make this easy. If you can guess how many birthdays I've had—within two—I'll leave you alone. But if you don't guess right, you have to go out with me."

Once, I felt sorry for myself for being born in a leap year, but in a bar, it gave me an advantage. At twenty years old, I'd only had five birthdays. It was a sure win—and more importantly, it got them laughing. And laughter opened doors.

As I liked to say: *"If you can't dazzle them with brilliance, baffle them with bullshit."*

It worked on Christine. We began dating.

Her family, as expected, was against it. Marrying outside your ethnicity wasn't tolerated, but I wasn't about to give up. *Plus, we're not going to get serious anyway, are we?*

We spent Sundays on the shores of Lake Ontario, where a bunch of guys played and the parties rolled. And then, once I was receiving a decent paycheck, I bought a brand-new 1963 Ford Falcon convertible—red, white top, black leather interior. It was my pride and joy, my first "four on the floor" V-6. From a family that always had used cars—or none at all—this was huge.

A week after my purchase, still excited, I invited Christine on a drive. I had several girls I could have invited, but since I had in mind to travel that day, I wanted to bring a *classy* girl. I drove Christine to my grandfather's place in Fredonia. It was my mother's dear grandpa Orlando, and while I'd never really had much of a relationship with him, I still tried to foster one by going to see him during my summers off school. Today, I was showing off my car, but he took one look at Christine and assumed I was there for his blessing to marry her. After all, I'd never brought a girl to visit him before. Christine was that kind of girl—educated, a nurse, beautiful inside and out. Of course, he thought it was a good idea.

As the miles drifted away upon our return trip, the exchange with Grandpa made me look at Christine differently than I had before. Until then, marriage was the last thing on my mind. But Christine wasn't like the other women I'd dated. She was someone I highly respected. Now that I had the eyes to see her differently, I fell for her, and fell hard. Most of my sisters, besides Terri, married for money, but I was marrying for love. I took that seriously.

Before long, I sold my drums to buy her a wedding ring. After years of weekend gigs, I knew bar life wouldn't work in a marriage. When Christine said yes, I was not only relieved—I was thrilled! We set a date.

I didn't have much money, but I had passion, and I poured it into her, into my work, and into our families. In both the Polish and Italian traditions, family was everything.

By the time the snow fell that year, my long winter commute from Niagara Falls and back was miserable. When I interviewed at Tops Market, closer to home, I negotiated hard. The director offered me $1.85 an hour. I said, "I need $2.05 an hour—I'm getting married."

He scoffed. I countered, my high school debate skills paying off:

"If you take care of me, I'll be with you for more than 45 years."

He gave me the wage I needed.

As an engaged couple, Christine and I spent nearly every Sunday with our families. Still, during our engagement, her mother tried to talk her out of marrying me. "He's a meat cutter, Christine. He'll never amount to anything!"

I had to give Christine's mom credit for being an exceptional cook. Whenever conversation got uncomfortable—which it often did—I would complement her cooking, and mean it wholeheartedly. The only thing Christine and I had going for us was that we were both Catholic, and it made the engagement somewhat smoother.

I had no idea that all the way up to the moment Christine was to walk with her father down the aisle, decorated with lovely spring flowers of hope, Christine's own Polish mother kept trying to talk her out of marrying "the filthy Italian." She told Christine that she would be stuck with a blue-collar guy for the rest of her life.

Fortunately for me, Christine didn't listen. That beautiful spring day in April 1964, my gorgeous, smart, practical nurse proudly walked down the aisle, with tears in her eyes, meeting my equally tearful ones. I had been taught that men weren't supposed to cry, but I felt overwhelmed with emotion. I finally felt wanted. When she took my hand in marriage, I set off to be the husband that her family didn't think I could be.

Of course, Chris and I knew it was a big challenge to bring our two disparate worlds together. I'll admit, when I found out that my new mother-in-law told my own mother the same thing she had told my bride, her words stung like barbed wire brushing bare skin—the kind of wound that doesn't bleed much but leaves a scar. I found it ironic that at only 19, I was already higher up the ladder than her husband, my father-in-law, who made feminine hygiene products at Kimberly-Clark.

I had to bite back my own cutting remarks when I realized the deeper place hers had come from. *I understand the burning desire a parent has to give their children a better life,* I said to myself, *so I can forgive them.* And I did.

For Christine, she'd been fighting her own battles. Her parents thought she must only be marrying me because she was pregnant—marrying me made no sense otherwise. She felt triumphant when she got her period on her wedding day and showed her mother the evidence. I was exonerated, though the timing wasn't ideal for our honeymoon. The good news? We made up for it quickly.

Married life pushed me toward maturity. Red had taught me honesty and integrity. Marriage taught me responsibility—sometimes more than I was ready for.

While hanging out as a married couple, I discovered you make different kinds of friends. Through our new friends, I met a guy by the name of Jim Engle, the branch manager of a bank.

"John, would you like to go to a Jaycee meeting?"

"Uh, sure?" But I was thinking, *What the hell is that?*

That's how I discovered the Junior Chamber of Commerce. Although still a butcher, I fancied myself a businessman, and the Jaycee model was "leadership training through community service." I didn't care much about that and hardly listened to their creed. Honestly, at first, I went for the social aspect, not the leadership training. But when I volunteered for a project, everything shifted.

Each year, the Niagara Falls aquarium hosted a special day for children with disabilities. I was assigned a group of kids with Down syndrome. These kids faced real struggles and bullying in the outside world, yet on that day, they were radiant—full of joy, free from judgment. Their palpable excitement stirred something inside of me. I felt it in every cell of my body. In this safe place, with no one to make fun of them, their faces and countenances were shining. I walked away with the greatest feeling inside... and it lingered for days.

At the next meeting, I truly listened to the Jaycee Creed for the first time:

We Believe:
That faith in God gives meaning
and purpose to human life;
That the brotherhood of man transcends
the sovereignty of nations;
That economic justice can best be won by
free men through free enterprise;
That government should be of laws rather than of men;
That earth's great treasure lies in human personality;
And that service to humanity is the best work of life.[5]

I was awestruck by the words, and something stirred in my soul.

5 Reprinted with permission by JCI National Organization, January 29, 2026.

To me, that was a prayer.

Plus, I'd just *lived* it with those kids. This creed became the foundation of my life. Every line had deep, rich meaning and purpose. I realized, *If we could only live like that today, it would be such a better world.*

From then on, I was all in. I volunteered for more projects, then even bigger ones. I had to figure out how to rally guys with different talents—sometimes guys I didn't even like—and inspire them to work together for free. It was my first real taste of management and human relations, and the lessons I learned there would be imprinted on me for life.

My proudest moment came in my second year, when I headed up the entire aquarium holiday. I had a big vision: Why not bring in the full aquarium experience as well as attractions from the Canadian side of the Falls, too? I loved working with the ineffable Mary Ellis Keleher, the aquarium's PR director, who saw what I saw and championed the cause with sponsors who could make this entire, fully magical day experience happen for these kids.

When Mary Ellis tragically passed away before the event, we renamed it in her honor: *The Keleher International Holiday for the Handicapped.* It became even more sacred to me then.

That year, Jaycee chapters from all over New York and Ontario joined in. Burger King—ironically foreshadowing my future—generously fed all the families. And when the dust settled, our project placed third nationally in the Junior Chamber awards under the youth project category.

I went on to become President of the Niagara Falls Jaycees. Along the way, I was named "JC of the Year" in my chapter, in the county, and in the state. I was even inducted into the publication *10 Outstanding Young Men of America* alongside legends like Bart Starr, Jim Ryun, and Arthur Ashe. Not bad company.

The Jaycees, however, gave me more than titles.

They gave me confidence, a sense of calling, and a creed I could live by. I wasn't just John Gullo anymore. I was John the Jaycee—and for the first time in my life, that was something I could not only stand behind but proudly stand in front of.

Life Lessons

At eighty-one, I can still recite the Jaycee Creed word for word. Names have come and gone, but those words remain. They were a touchpoint, a catalyst, a guide.

Harry Truman once said, "It is amazing what you can accomplish if you do not care who gets the credit."

When I first joined, I went back to one of my high school teachers, Mr. Falsetti, for advice. He told me, "John, just be yourself. You're funny, and when you make fun of yourself, everyone laughs. You don't need big words to speak. Being yourself is enough."

From then on, I spoke my truth, like Red, without pretending to be anyone else.

And Christine—she was the blessing I never saw coming. I wasn't even looking, and yet, she opened my eyes to love, respect, and partnership. She changed my life in ways I never could have imagined.

"John has no barriers, and sometimes that
gets that gets you in trouble. But overall,
there's no question what John believes, what he thinks."
– Robert Bell, Owner of Bell Printing

CHAPTER 5:

Humor in Service

"A person without a sense of humor is like a wagon without springs. It's jolted by every pebble on the road."
– Henry Ward Beecher

The Jaycee Creed turned out to be a guiding light. Up until then, I had witnessed so much mafia involvement in church and business that it seemed normal, if not inevitable—just part of the streets of Buffalo and other neighborhoods. My brother stayed tied up with that malevolent world for a while, and while Mom swore he moved on, I was never sure if he ever fully left it behind.

The Jaycees saved me from myself—and from my upbringing. They gave me a new lens through which to view all the colors of life and contribution. Suddenly, I was rubbing shoulders with guys who had professional careers. At every meeting, I learned something smart or empowering, and before I knew it, "John the Jaycee" was reshaping my character. Somewhere in there, I even became... fun. I hadn't let myself be so fun since jumping out of the school window to pick a bouquet of daisies. Now I could be fun... in a *constructive* way.

I needed that outlet. As the saying goes, "Laugh and the whole world laughs with you, cry and you cry alone." I decided to laugh.

I came out of my shell, gained confidence, and let my natural sense of humor and personality shine. I'd always been good at remembering and telling jokes, but now I realized humor could do more than entertain. It could connect people, soften tensions, and make hard work easier.

Soon, I was channeling that humor into Jaycee events. One March, I pitched an Irish Wake for our St. Patrick's Day social. And remember—this was the 1960s, when people thought Dean Martin's drinking jokes were family entertainment, and nobody had heard of political correctness. So, what did we do? We built a coffin, borrowed a mannequin from the department store, and staged the whole thing at the restaurant where we held our monthly meetings. They served green beer with corned beef and cabbage, and we set the coffin on display with a marker that read:

"Here lies Katie O'Day, violated by an Irishman in the year of our Lord 1950."

Now, if you wrote that on a placard today, you'd have the HR department, the mayor's office, and probably the FBI on your doorstep by morning. But back then, everybody howled as they walked through the door—because it was meant as slapstick, a bit of gallows humor in the Irish tradition.

And the kicker? Their raffle ticket was part of the gag. The grand prize? With a dramatic drumroll, I announced:

"The winner has to store the coffin until next year!"

The place exploded with laughter, and sure enough, the poor winner had that coffin delivered to their home the very next day. It became a Jaycee tradition that carried on for years.

When the state Jaycees held their convention to honor the Ten Outstanding Young Men of New York, I wanted Niagara Falls to host. My team and I hit the road with our bid package. That's when I dreamed up the "Mafia-style" promotion.

We rented a limousine and dressed six of us like mobsters. At every chapter stop, I gave my serious, professional pitch—and then deadpanned that the reason our package was so cheap was thanks to our sponsor: *The Mothers and Fathers of Italian Americans*. I never spelled it out. I just let "MAFIA" dawn on them slowly.

Then I introduced Guido, one of our real Italian members, in a black shirt and white tie. With his thick New York accent, he gave a deadpan welcome on behalf of "the sponsors." Finally, our planted heckler in the crowd stood and shouted:

"Hey! Aren't you part of organized crime?"

Guido pulled out a starter pistol and shot him on the spot. Our plant in the audience collapsed dramatically while Guido tucked away the gun, looked coolly over the crowd, and asked:

"Any more questions?"

You've never seen a room erupt with more nervous laughter in your life. And to this day, it remains for people an unforgettable event.

Life Lessons

Humor became one of my most valuable tools in business and in life. I used the "Mothers and Fathers of Italian Americans" gag more than once. My wife worried I might be asking for trouble from the *real* mafia—but I was never threatened, not once.

When I served as Sergeant of Arms at the Ogden Rotary Club in Utah years later, I dusted off Guido myself. I showed up in a black shirt and white tie, rocking on my heels, fingers laced like a patient godfather while I did my spiel.

I said in a heavy Italian dialect, "Some of yous guys come late; some of yous talk; some of yous guys come early. Now I'm with the Mothers and Fathers of Italian Americans and we sell insurance. If you're going to do them things, you gotta give me some money."

Right on cue, my plant in the audience raised his hand nervously to ask if we represented organized crime. *Bang!* One more fake body hit the floor. One more room roared.

Over those two years, humor turned meetings into memories and colleagues into friends.

Looking back, I actually find it hilarious that local legend has it that Ogden's 25th Street, just down the road from where the Rotary meets, had once been one of the most dangerous mob haunts in the country. They say Capone himself refused to stay there—it was too rough, even for him! Now that's sayin' somethin'.[6] It wasn't your typical Mormon neighborhood.

By the time I arrived, the place had cleaned itself up, and later my foundation even helped build a safe, educational venue for kids nearby. To be able to provide to children safety and education I never got as a kid meant the world to me. I was lucky enough to have a couple of great mentors—and maybe they could have a fighting chance to make something of themselves, too.

"When I read a book or see a movie, I want a takeaway. Something that teaches me. With John, it's clearly his heart for people. What he has given up to advance people, to speak into people's lives... He was very gracious with his time, his energy, his money. He was selfless. He didn't have to do any of that. That's just John."

– Rick Cowley, Burger King franchisee

6 Kim Bowsher, "A History of Violence: Ogden's 25th Street," *Utah Stories*, August 29, 2014, https://utahstories.com/2014/08/a-history-of-violence-ogdens-25th-street/

CHAPTER 6:

The Making of a Family

"Fathering is not something perfect men do, but something that perfects the man."
– Frank Pittman

I came from a generation where a man was supposed to do "X" and a woman was supposed to do "Y." Tradition shaped both Christine's Polish upbringing and my Italian one. Then we added our own personalities into the mix.

What I found in Christine was security—someone to care for me and someone I wanted to care for in return. On the day we married, my tears were real. Her mother may have thought I was just a common laborer, but she didn't know how seriously I took my commitment, nor how career-driven I already was. Especially now, with something so important to work for.

I worked long overtime hours to get ahead. Christine understood and supported me, but my in-laws never did, to my dismay. Once, when my father-in-law was giving me the third degree for all my overtime, I asked if he'd rather I came home and went bowling with the guys or hung out at the bar drinking. He gave me no answer. Maybe because that was *his* lifestyle.

I moved up through the ranks quickly at Tops Markets, eventually supervising four meat departments. But the grocery business was brutal. Fifty-hour weeks were standard, with no relief or extra training to further you personally or professionally. It could chew you up and spit you out.

In those early years, Christine dreamed of a large family, like the ones we came from. I agreed—and as a passionate Sicilian, I didn't exactly mind what that required. Our physical relationship was vital to me.

But heartbreak came in the night, too. Our first pregnancy ended in miscarriage. Then Christine carried twin girls to seven months. Just as we were getting ready to celebrate bringing them home, they were born prematurely. One died during birth and was never named. The other lived only a single day, but New York law required a full burial: coffin, gravesite, the works. I had to handle all those details. Christine was in the hospital, and I tried to be strong.

That night, I broke down. I sobbed until morning, repeating our baby's name over and over again, *"Maria, Maria."* Then I pulled myself together, walked into that hospital, and stood strong for Christine. I thought that's what a man was supposed to do. What I didn't know was that burying my grief for her sake would harm our marriage. By the time I admitted how deeply it had hurt me, decades had passed.

To make matters worse, when I was trying to be strong during Christine's and my darkest hours, then came the cruelty. My seething mother-in-law told me I was going to kill her daughter—just as she claimed my sister had driven her own husband to suicide. I swallowed those words whole, never repeating them to my wife. I kept the peace for Christine's sake, kept showing up for family events, and over time, her mother's outbursts faded. I never got an apology, but I forgave, again and again.

Meanwhile, every pregnancy pushed Christine through her own private hell. When she became pregnant again, I went to work each day, holding my breath, praying God would grant us a child. At seven months, it was nearly sheer agony.

Then our son Johnny was born. It felt like the light of God shone upon him as the doctor delivered him right into Christine's arms. I felt as if life suddenly made sense. I tucked my grief over my girls safely away in my heart and focused on this blessed moment. What a joy to have a bouncing baby boy! Johnny became my world. I couldn't wait to get home from work to pick him up and hold him and enjoy the hell out of that little guy. I loved the way his eyes danced, and he was beloved by his grandparents and family.

I learned a lot during that time about the "circle of life." My sweet sister Jackie contracted cancer at age 33. It was so quick that in seven days she was gone, and we were all in shock. My other anchor, Terri, had been working for Ashton Oil and learned computers in the very early days. GM hired her because of this special skillset, then promoted her and moved her to GM in Michigan. There, she met and fell in love with Bob. I was happy for her but knew she would not be coming home to New York again.

Christine and I experienced the hope of another pregnancy, only to lose it. It was bitter irony: Christine was a licensed practical nurse, working for three of the best gynecologists in Niagara Falls. None could help. My sister Joanne, who had suffered three miscarriages of her own, found hope with a specialist who bluntly told her, "You're trying too hard. Adopt first." She adopted, then went on to give birth to two sons. So, we went to see the same specialist.

He was arrogant, with no bedside manner whatsoever. "If I take you on as a patient, you'll do *everything* I say. No exceptions." We reluctantly agreed. He skimmed Christine's file for thirty seconds and then grinned.

"This isn't fertility. Your husband could probably knock up every woman on the block!"

He chuckled, ignoring my wife's grimace. "Your history shows your uterus doesn't gain strength as the pregnancy advances. That's why you carried twins so long—they don't gain weight until later. The fix is simple: get pregnant, I'll sew up your cervix, put you on bed rest, and you'll carry to term."

Crude and arrogant as he was, he was right. Christine carried to full term. Our second son, Danny, was born via C-section—a five-year-younger miracle.

Christine was blissful with her newborn. As the months passed, however, she told me she couldn't bear the thought of enduring more pregnancy trauma and had her tubes tied. I honored her decision. We became a family of four—and we didn't take either of those miracle children for granted. I worked long hours to make sure she could stay home as much as possible. She quit her job for a time, and I got to watch as my wife blossomed, excelling as both a mother and a partner.

At first, we rented a two-bedroom apartment, with heat included for $150 a month. Soon, we bought our first house in Niagara Falls for $8,400, then another in the LaSalle area for $12,000, after I'd been promoted again at Tops Market to department manager. We lived simply—family, friends, Sundays together.

Meanwhile, I learned from mentors like Burt Moore, my supervisor. He was Canadian; he was brilliant but had his quirks. He bewildered me often, especially when sometimes in mid-conversation, he'd just walk away. Finally, I was fed up.

"Why the hell are you walking away when we're deep in conversation?"

"In management," he said, "you need people to *wonder* how close you are to others. Walking away keeps them guessing." I thought it was nonsense, but eventually I saw the strategy. He didn't want to play favorites.

I was thriving, but Tops operated on a corporate bonus system. One year, despite my success, the company underperformed. No bonus. Burt grinned at me.

"Look at the bright side," he said. "Everything you did will go on your record. You still get credit."

I deadpanned back, "That's funny. I put 'credit' on the table for my family last night, and they said it tasted awful."

Then I walked away.

I found out my brother Jim was getting a divorce, and it saddened me. He blew it off, as if it was no big deal. He'd stepped away from many of his shady deals and bars, and it seemed like he was thriving in the restaurant business. He'd bought into the Henry's Drive-In chain as a restaurant owner, and it was going well. He let me know when he had the chance to buy five restaurants, and I was elated when he called me.

"Want to be my partner? I'll put the business in your name, so it won't affect my divorce."

Suddenly, I was simultaneously relieved and over the moon. To get to work with my brother? Amazing! I had been growing more and more disillusioned with Tops. Besides, family was everything. In my mind, it was a no-brainer.

"Hell, yes!" I said.

Immediately, Christine and I moved to Kenmore with the boys. Johnny was in elementary school and thriving. Danny was a toddler, and he and Christine became very close as I worked long, long hours, with only Sundays off.

This is for them, I told myself. I believed it, and I built and strived, then built and strived some more.

Then one day, Jim called me in. My dad, Red, happened to be there, too, and I was delighted to be with them both until I noticed the smirk on Jim's face. I had seen that before… a lot, in fact, when I was growing up, and the same look when he talked about his former wife. My heart fell.

"John," he said, that same smirk about his lips, "you're being let go."

"What the hell are you talking about?"

"My divorce is final," he said. "And now you're fired." Then he looked at Dad. "John will never amount to anything. He doesn't have common business sense."

I couldn't even look at Red's face. I didn't see his reaction when I slammed out the door.

It cut deep. Bad enough to be fired by my brother, worse to be dismissed like that in front of my father and mentor.

Although the corporation was in my name, Jim had never issued stock to me. He controlled it all. He knew he could use me, and he did. I worked my ass off to run those restaurants well and right, and he was only using me for my name on the paperwork until it was convenient to fire me.

Soon, my brother remarried. And I was left with *nothing*. I was bitter—and for good reason. For a time, if I saw Jim's fancy cars at a family gathering, I just stayed outside while my wife and kids went in to enjoy family. I couldn't face him. I was afraid of what I would do.

Eventually, I realized this avoidance only hurt my parents. I swallowed my rage and went inside.

And, for the first time in my life, I collected unemployment. That wasn't me.

Very quickly, I answered a blind ad for a meat supervisor. Turns out it was Tops Market again! I returned, this time overseeing four departments in Niagara County. My new boss, Nino Nanula, was a sharp Italian man who taught me one of the greatest lessons in retail:

"Trust is earned by few.
Always expect the worst, and
Be surprised by the best."

Financially, it was better than unemployment, but the long hours left Christine carrying the parenting role alone yet again. I tried to make up for it: an above-ground pool, basketball hoop, weekend playtime. Those hours I spent with my wife and children were precious to me, absolutely precious. But I was gone too much. By 1971, I was making $18,000 a year, which was a solid salary then, but I was often working eighty-hour weeks.

Finally, I told Christine, "I have to make a change. I'm going to gamble—and I have to win."

Life Lessons

Facing so much hardship didn't break me—it shaped me. It made me resilient. I came to realize, as an adult, that I don't hit brick walls the way most people do. Most hit that wall and stop; I hit it, bounce off, and redirect myself in the trajectory *I* choose.

Every challenge, I've learned, carries an opportunity. That same mindset became vital in business—minimizing losses, maximizing gains. I discovered there was no such thing as bad business, only bad management. With time, I saw that a good manager could work his way out of almost anything... provided he had enough capital.

Later in New York State, when I needed cash for the operations of a business, there was a usury law: no credit card company could charge more than 12% interest. I had three cards. I'd use one, then the next, then the next—cycling through until I had $12,000 in play without paying interest. I share that strategy while I tell my grandkids today: "Problems create opportunities. Too many people stop and quit. Don't quit."

Christine and I would stay married for the next two decades. She did what was considered a woman's role in those times, and I did what I thought was mine. But we never really shared our feelings. We hadn't been taught how. Red gave me some great advice about talking after sex. "You're done, but she's just getting started on the intimacy." It was about as close as I ever came to being taught how to honor a woman's point of view. It wasn't part of our culture, our schools, our Catechism, or our society.

That's why now, I spend a lot of time telling my grandchildren—and anyone who will listen—how crucial *real* communication is in marriage. Two-way communication is the root of everything good and healthy. A few years ago, at a family retreat, I told my grandkids: *"Talk to your spouse. Keep the lines of communication open. Every couple will fight, but if you're mad, give it a day or two. Then say, 'Honey, remember the other day? I felt hurt by what you said.' Don't push it down or ignore it, but don't lash out in the heat of the moment either. That only leads to bad feelings and words you'll regret."*

I also tell them: "It's not a failure to go to therapy. It's healthy. Work on solving the small problems before they grow into big ones."

"If we hit a wall, John always comes back with ideas. And a lot of them are great—ones that nobody ever thought about before. His example teaches us how to not look and see boxes, but how to take a problem and figure it out. I don't think John's ever hit the wall. I don't think he's ever stopped. There's always a solution."
– Mike Leatham, owner of SymbolArts

PART II
Growth & Opportunity

"Success is not the key to happiness.
Happiness is the key to success.
If you love what you are doing,
you will be successful."
– Albert Schweitzer

CHAPTER 7:

An Ordinary Man... Extraordinary Risks

"I can promise you this... there was a hand in my life.
I look back at so many things in my life, and it wasn't me...
so many blessings happened, and I had to pinch myself.
I'm like, 'I'm just an ordinary Joe'."
– Henry Marsh, Olympian, Hall of Famer,
breaker of four U.S. Steeplechase records

I couldn't take it anymore. My work ethic was unshakable, but the long hours in the grocery business were wearing me down. I had worked my way up the ladder—cleanup boy, apprentice meat cutter, then meat cutter, department manager, and finally supervisor over six departments after I was fired from my brother's employ, but success didn't feel like success. I hated my job.

When Chris and I sat down and really talked, she told me what I already knew: my skills were being wasted. She agreed to return to nursing for a while so I could take a gamble. I promised her it would be short-term—and with her blessing, I took the biggest risk of my career. I walked away from groceries and joined Burger King Corporation, also known as BK Corp.

In 1971, Burger King had just been bought by Pillsbury. They were reorganizing, growing aggressively, and splitting the company into new divisions under three vice presidents. Buffalo, where I applied, had only six company stores but was primed for expansion. Loaded with confidence because of my time working with Jim on "our" restaurants, I answered a newspaper ad and was hired as a night manager for $8,500 a year—a $10,000 pay cut. The hours were brutal, but Chris kept her promise, and I kept mine.

They assigned me to Burger King on Niagara Falls Boulevard. The manager, Jim Harrison, was slim, intellectual, organized—the complete opposite of me, who preferred to run things on the fly. After six weeks, I was promoted to first assistant manager, then within a few months, to manager of a store in North Tonawanda. They could see my hard work, my hours of commitment, and my commitment to the restaurant's success. I just never gave up—I only got smarter.

The best part? Chris could finally leave night shifts behind and focus on being a mom again. She was incredible at it! I noticed our boys absolutely *thrived* under her attention and affection. Together, we were a great team.

Tonawanda was a small-volume store, so I hustled to drum up business. I plastered cars in parking lots with BOGO coupons. I got permission to remodel the tired old restaurant—ceiling, walls, fresh paint, new graphics—and rallied the staff to pitch in. The crew and volunteers were proud of how classy it looked. I was impressed with *them*. Back in those days, people did shit like that—they took pride in their establishment and their own contribution.

Morale went up. Sales went up. Management noticed.

For once, I wasn't just grinding—I was in the right place at the right time, and everything was shining.

Promotions followed quickly. Within several months, I was transferred to another store on Union Boulevard. This time, my commute was 30 minutes compared to a few, so I had to add that to the hours I was already working. Within eighteen months, I was running my own brand-new store on Sheridan Boulevard. The commute was even longer, traffic was a pain, but I was thrilled. I was finally living the dream, even if the hours were long and weekends were reserved for family get-togethers before heading back to the grind.

I had a knack for spotting talent in my crew and promoting them into management. I loved watching people rise. It was making all of us successful! Then came my first big test.

A franchise restaurant in Olean, New York, lost its operator at the last minute. Corporate scrambled and asked me to step in. Olean was eighty miles from home, and I had to leave Chris and the boys for a solid month. It hurt, but I told Chris, "This could be good for us." She backed me without hesitation. I poured everything I had and everything I was into that store. I trained the employees on cleanliness and customer service. I marketed like crazy, and the Olean store's opening broke sales records! It built my reputation.

Soon after, Burger King created a new position: Franchise District Manager for Western Pennsylvania and upstate New York. Nobody else wanted it—too much travel, too uncertain a path. I took it. Nine franchisees, eleven stores, nearly 70,000 miles a year on the company car. I was gone Monday to Friday, but the pay was better, and my wife stood behind me. I never took her support for granted.

My first big challenge came in Pittsburgh with a franchisee named Hal Alleto. He ran four high-volume restaurants, but customers hated the new "hospitality system" with three cash registers. Orders backed up. The line was interminable. People walked out.

I convinced Hal to try to modify the new system (similar to what you'd see at McDonald's today, but no one knew of it then). The old "Indian Trail" system of big orders being pulled aside while being filled, keeping all the smaller orders moving at the same time. Customers loved it. Lines moved rapidly. Sales jumped. But Corporate hadn't approved it.

When VP Roger Swift came to town and saw it, he lit into me.

I stood my ground.

"Just wait until you see the numbers." I wasn't kidding.

Hal also had a big mouth and fiery attitude. Once, after he tried blaming me for something, I shot back, "If I know something that can help you and you won't listen, you're not as smart as you think you are."

Then I walked out.

That did it—he started listening. Eventually, Hal told me, "You're too smart for this job. Go open your own restaurant. When you do, I'll finally change my signs to the new Burger King logo."

"I'll take you up on it!" I warned and grinned at him. I began enjoying this man as a friend and valued him highly in my life. *At some point,* I thought, *I might even listen to his wisdom, too*!

The work kept stretching me, and so did my reputation. I opened a new store in Rochester with three young, New York City partners who'd heard of me: Larry Kessler, a Wall Street powerhouse; Chuck Bidane, a Yale tennis star; and Norm Weinstein, whose wealthy father had bankrolled him. Their business name was Northern Trinity Restaurants, which I found totally ironic since all three were Jewish. They were sharp, funny, and taught me things I never would have learned otherwise. Larry, in particular, took me aside and schooled me on money. "It's not how much you're making when you're making money," he told me. "It's how much you're not making while you're making money." He showed me the ropes of tax law and business finance—completely legal, but mind-blowing for a kid with no formal schooling in that arena.

We had plenty of funny and hilarious moments along the way. For one, our grand opening turned out to be on a Jewish holiday, so guess who the only guy who opened the restaurant was? A month later, Chuck was washing trays in the big industrial sink. Here he was, a big owner and hand-washing trays. I teased him: "Did you ever picture yourself at Yale, thinking someday you'd be scrubbing away at a sink at Burger King—and loving it?"

He cracked up and his grin was wide... even as he finished the trays.

Later, when Larry and I attended a national convention, VP Ramon Morale said in his Cuban accent, "You guys need to know

Burger King is poised…" Larry leaned over and whispered, "I can't believe he's talking about us—'Jew' guys!" We laughed until we cried.

Burger King still hadn't come up with a job description for Franchise District Manager, so each of us in that position just had to create on the fly as we went, lending our expertise in Ops & Mgt. In my opinion, that meant supporting the franchisees in any way that we knew how.

Not every store was smooth. The Watertown opening was a disaster in the making: the new electric broiler failed, the freezer broke down, I had to stash product in a nearby grocery store, and the weather was notoriously brutal. We made it work, but Corporate decided to make me the scapegoat. They hauled me to the corporate office in Miami, accusing me of having "a problem with the salesman" who had supplied all of the large appliances. You see, Davmore was a subsidiary of BK, and they supplied all the equipment for the restaurants at that time. That ticked me off because the equipment failed. The truth was, the company wasn't supporting the franchise properly. It wouldn't have mattered who the Burger King appliance salesperson was! I was mad at the company's policies that kept their franchises from being successful, and I knew we could do better.

Later that year, Burger King announced the first-ever Franchise District Manager training in Miami. They gathered us all together—and one night, in front of everyone, the three vice presidents zeroed in on me. I was no dummy.

I saw this coming a mile away, I thought. They weren't just talking to me; they were trying to make an example of me.

"There's lots of things I've learned from John, but one is, you got to go after what you want. I've never been able to take the risk that he takes. He's definitely got the ability. To get rich, you just have to save money. To get really rich, you have to take a lot of risks."

– Trent Christofferson, Financial Planner

CHAPTER 8:

Leadership Means Innovation

"A true leader has the confidence to stand alone, the courage to make tough decisions, and the compassion to listen to the needs of others. He does not set out to be a leader, but becomes one by the equality of his actions and the integrity of his intent."
– Douglas MacArthur

"Gentlemen, hopefully you can see by my track record that I am a loyal guy. But let me ask you something," I said, speaking plainly but respectfully, in front of the whole Franchise Manager Training team—since they'd started it. "Where does loyalty to the company end, and credibility with a franchisee become the most important choice? This is your bread and butter, fellas."

They stared back at me, brows raised, mouths open. Burger King was still so green in the franchise business that nobody had a straight answer. Finally, I drove it home. "Blow your loyalty a little, fine. But lose credibility with a franchisee? You've lost everything. It's your job to make them successful."

That philosophy followed me everywhere, and not always quietly. At Burger King's first convention, I sat one evening with a mix of franchisees and execs. Jerry Bishop was there—the franchisee genius behind the shorter service line we'd rolled out to great success. I liked Jerry and respected his ideas. However, when the Vice President of Engineering puffed out his chest and told the franchisees, "Everybody should be doing this!" I couldn't keep quiet.

"You're wrong," I told him flatly, in front of the whole group. "It needs more work before we dump it on all franchisees. Each store is different."

The next morning, Roger Swift, Burger King's VP, pulled me aside with my area manager, Arnold Hyatt. Roger's face was red. "What the hell are you doing, John? Telling a vice president he was wrong—in front of franchisees?"

Arnold jumped in before I could. "Roger, what did you expect John to do? Agree with someone who's wrong and lose credibility with franchisees? That doesn't work. I'm with John—he's right. Franchisee trust comes first."

Roger huffed, but he knew Arnold had a point. Jerry and I patched things up easily. We both wanted improvements that worked, not credit for half-baked ideas. Our friendship grew stronger, and not long after, Jerry and I talked about Burger King's new idea: a drive-thru.

At the time, most Americans had never even heard of such a thing. Together, we prepped the first one in Rome, New York, in 1974. I knew it would take more than construction—it needed neighborhood education. On opening day, I staged the show. Three employees, in their own cars, looped through the drive-thru again and again, pretending to be customers. Locals passing by stopped, gawked, and thought, *Well, if it's good enough for them...* Within hours, the fake line turned into a real one. *VOILA*! The drive-thru was born, and Burger King was never the same.

Around that time, Jerry also introduced décor themes beyond the cookie-cutter dining rooms that were the norm for all new restaurants, and I was the one to implement them. Piece by piece, I was building a reputation for doing "the next right thing." Arnold Hyatt put it plainly: "John, it's not about having a spotless reputation. It's about having a name that people know. Even if you stumble, you've got to be out there."

That stuck with me. Pleasing Corporate was impossible, but making franchisees successful—that was a hill I'd die on.

In 1975, Burger King hit warp speed when Carol's Restaurants—a 150-store regional chain—decided to convert to Burger King. That meant a hundred remodels in my backyard. My determination to make restaurants successful had me buzzing, and Corporate backed me in writing: *"John Gullo is thoroughly versed in all aspects of Burger King construction, equipment, and décor. He is authorized to make field decisions."*

That was a career-changing memo. It gave me the authority to make calls on the fly, and believe me, I used it. When Carol's architects cut corners—like trying to skip the 2x10 beam system that gave Burger Kings their trademark look—I flat-out refused. Their architect even flew a piece of the beam to Miami to complain to Burger King's head architect. Roger Swift, to his credit, backed me. The standard held. Decades later, the Carol's part of the franchise would sell for over $1 billion. Who knew the company I'd once wrestled into compliance would become such a powerhouse?

Of course, it wasn't all smooth sailing. In Pittsburgh, a wealthy franchisee tinkered with product prep across his stores. I told him, "Fine, but at least make it consistent so customers don't notice the difference."

That got me hauled down to headquarters in Miami once again. The verdict? "Back off, John." Corporate only cared about opening more stores, not about operations. That was an early lesson in what drove the company—growth first, quality later. I didn't agree, so I had to work quality in, wherever I could.

That same year, growth was swamping us, and Corporate didn't always like my politics. That year, BK decided that they wanted all Franchise DMs to serve as company DMs. It was to establish a "correct" career path for HR. I ended up swapping districts with Jim Harrison. He took my franchise territory while I managed company stores in Buffalo. It felt like a demotion to me, but it introduced me to Tom Mueller, a restaurant manager so good I often sent prospective franchisees to him just to see what a top-notch operation looked like! Tom's motto mirrored my own: "Just do it right. Then do the next right thing." It renewed my faith in humankind and business.

At a later convention, Olympian Henry Marsh gave advice that sent shivers down my spine: "Ask yourself, is this problem worth a stress-induced heart attack? The answer is always no." Wise words. I stopped sweating some of the small stuff.

In 1976, Don Szabo, the same Pittsburgh franchisee I once butted heads with, asked me, "John, have you ever wanted to open your own restaurant? You're built for this."

"Nothing ventured, nothing gained," I said, only half-joking. Then I studied him for a moment. *Is he serious?* I had only been with Burger King for about four and a half years. Hal had mentioned this to me prior, but to *really* think of becoming a business owner, a franchisee was mind-blowing. Yet name after name from my BK rolodex came back to me. Jim Harrison, Arnold Hyatt, Roger Swift, and Bill O'Donnell had all stepped away from Corporate to take the plunge.

I was only thirty-one, not exactly flush with cash, and I hardly came from a family of investors. But Don said he wanted to introduce me to a partner with money, someone who wanted me as the operator. Enter Malcom Kennedy Jr.—a feisty Irishman, ex–NFL Players Association Director, casino promoter, charming, connected, and, by his own admission, half genius and half disaster.

We met for eight hours straight in a Buffalo motel lobby and hit it off instantly. I discovered another amazing thing about Malcom as we talked. In the early days of professional football, players didn't make much at all. They were dirt poor, barely scraping by. Malcom had stepped into the gap as the very first director of the National Football League Players Association. He was the one who pushed for players to get real money through sponsorships. When the Teamsters tried to unionize the association, the NFLPA decided to form its own union instead, and Mal hired a professional, Ed Garvey, to take over as executive director. Mal was the instrument who got NFL players paid like professionals, and he wore his NFL ring with the kind of pride that made you sit up straighter when you shook his hand.

He admitted freely that he was a great promoter but, in his own words, sometimes a lousy businessman. He had hit rock-bottom failures and then turned around and scored wild successes. I was already impressed, but then he told me about a venture he and a couple of guys with no money had pulled together—a little idea called the Marina Hotel-Casino, which would later become the MGM Grand. It had opened just the year before, in 1975, and this was the project funding his new ventures at the time. Mal wasn't just dabbling—he was the kind of man who could turn nothing into something, and then into an empire.

Before he flew back to Las Vegas, he made me an offer. I liked the guy so much, and respected him even more. But still I said, "I'm not sure, and I definitely need to discuss this with my wife, but I will certainly consider your offer."

That evening, I went home to the laughter of Johnny and Danny and their friends, all of them soaking in the last days of summer before school began. Johnny was eleven, Danny was six, and I loved how different they were from one another. Watching them with their buddies, I felt a tug in my chest. If I stayed on my current path, the way my career was catapulting upward, the next stop was Burger King's corporate headquarters. But with my management style, could I really spend half my time doing the job and the other half covering my ass like so many guys in Corporate? My answer was an honest *hell no*. Christine felt the same way about my career trajectory.

So, I took Mal's offer, and together we applied for a franchise.

The timing couldn't have been more comical. That same weekend, I was clowning around on a 20-inch bike with the boys, showing off like I was still a kid myself. I popped a wheelie, threw out my foot to break my fall, and—SQUELCH! Excruciating pain tore through me. I looked down in shock to see my toes pointing backward. My ankle had twisted a full 180 degrees.

At the hospital, the swelling was so bad they couldn't operate, so they slapped me in a full leg cast and sent me home to wait it out. I was miserable. I didn't know how not to work, how to sit still. It wasn't in my DNA.

Then Monday morning, the phone rang. It was Burger King. "We have an opportunity for you as an upcoming franchisee to open a restaurant... in Brownsville, Texas, or Logan, Utah."

I sat there staring at the phone, overwhelmed. I'd never been west of Chicago. The only concept I had of "the West" came from Bonanza reruns and John Wayne flicks, with a little Clint Eastwood and Blazing Saddles mixed in.

Texas might have been the easy call, but I sent Chris to the library to dig into Logan, Utah. She came back with books and brochures about the state's natural beauty, family values, conservative politics, and that mix of snow and heat we already knew, though the dry climate would be new. It was nothing like I'd pictured when we filled out the franchise application.

But then I thought about what we were facing in New York. At Danny's elementary school, a first-grader had just been arrested for selling drugs. *What the hell? A first-grader?* The welfare system seemed out of control to me. The city cut library hours down to three half-days just to keep the lights on. We were raising our boys in a run-down, racially segregated, economically depressed environment where even the national news was bleak—Vietnam still raging, the president facing impeachment.

I turned to Chris. "We live in hell. It can't be worse than this." She nodded, and I added, "You know, Chris, this could be really great for our family." We were both worried about leaving family, but in my mind, the dreams for what we could create together swam in my eyes.

The decision was made. We were on to new adventures, and the West was our new frontier.

Looking back, I realize that meeting Malcom wasn't just about opening restaurants—it was about learning how to dream bigger than I thought possible. He taught me to spot opportunities, to take risks, to promote ideas people didn't yet understand, and to have the guts to make them work. Those same lessons, first tested in the restaurant business, would come back to me decades later when I found myself doing something nobody had heard of yet—pickleball. I couldn't have known it then, but the seeds of my future were planted in those early conversations with Mal.

Lessons to Live By

When I first met Malcolm Kennedy Jr., I had no idea the kind of partnership in store. The man's connections, skill sets, and brilliant brain left me in awe. But Malcolm also knew something most visionaries forget: he wasn't brilliant at everything. He taught me one of the most valuable lessons of my life—hire out your weaknesses.

It was a blessing, and sometimes a curse. Malcolm didn't always want to see when something wasn't working, but he valued my insight and ideas. More than anything, he respected what he called my integrity. That meant the world to me.

Football wasn't his only arena. He'd been general chairman of the U.S. Olympic boxing team during the Pan Am trials in 1975, the year before I met him. He was also secretary-treasurer of the U.S. Amateur Boxing Federation, founder of the Wisconsin Sports Hall of Fame in Madison, and executive director of the National 1,000 Yard Club of Menasha.

Malcolm poured his energy into everything he touched, and through him I learned that no matter what the field—sports, business, or something brand new—you can always leave a positive mark. Who would've guessed that after he passed, his legacy would inspire me to help launch a sport hardly anyone had heard of in the early 2000s?

Malcolm also wasn't impressed with the so-called "high society" or ivory-tower academia. He believed, like General George Patton, "If a man does his best, what else is there?" But like me, he was also driven to be accepted. Despite his law degree from UW, he never cracked the inner circle of the elite. Once, the manager of a university fundraising campaign wouldn't even give him the time of day.

When the campaign came up short, Malcolm wrote a check that put them just over the top, just enough to hit 100%, simply to tick the athletic director off. That was Malcolm: never bitter, never needy, but never afraid to prove a point with flair.

The "elite" may never have accepted him. But the rest of us—athletes, business colleagues, friends—loved him. And I was proud to be among them.

"Years ago, when I worked with John, he always said, 'Do the right thing. Then the next right thing.' Years later, when I had a chance to work for Dave Thomas, late in my career at Wendy's, Dave would say, 'Just do the right thing'—just like John."
– Tom Mueller, former Burger King Vice President, former Wendy's President

CHAPTER 9:

From Franchise Manager to Franchisee

"The American West is just arriving at the threshold of its greatness and growth. Where the West of yesterday is glamorized in our fiction, the future of the American West now is both fabulous and factual."
– Lyndon B. Johnson

Signing on with Malcom Kennedy Jr. was a dream come true—but it almost didn't happen.

When Don Smith left McDonald's and became the new President of Burger King in the late '70s, he quickly put a lid on the gold rush. Too many company men were leaving to become franchisees. His fix was a rule never implemented before: no one could leave Corporate to become a franchisee until they'd put in *a full five years* with Corporate. That was a problem. I'd only logged four and a half years. Plus, I was on disability to boot, hobbling around in a cast.

I understood Don's bind. Franchisees needed talent, but if Burger King lost too many experienced operators, the company's growth would stall. As growth remained their number one goal, he couldn't close the door completely to franchisees, but he could at least slow the bleeding.

Fortunately for me, Jerry Winters—the new VP who replaced Roger Swift—liked me. Jerry would one day become a franchisee himself, but at that time, he was still in Corporate, and he approved the application that Malcom and I submitted. By the time I was up and moving again in my walking cast, I had technically crossed the five-year mark. The door opened.

Between Brownsville, Texas, and Logan, Utah, I chose Utah because I could smell opportunity. At that point, there was only one Burger King in the whole state, down in a tiny "metropolis" called Provo. If we succeeded, the field for expansion was wide open.

Malcom and I formed our first partnership, Northwest Foods Limited—or NFL, as he liked to call it. He loved keeping the NFL moniker so he could flash his ring without explanation. We started with four partners in total, including Don.

In November of 1975, I flew out to Utah in my walking cast. As the plane descended, the mountains took my breath away. I'd grown up around wooded hills and flatlands; this was a wall of rock and sky, 12,000 feet high. Driving north from the Salt Lake City Airport, the Wasatch Front unfolded alongside me, ridge after ridge. Then I cut off at Brigham City, climbed the canyon road, and found myself in Cache Valley. There were lakes, deep green meadows, and open land with a history of fur trappers caching supplies, furs, and money in hollow logs—some never living long enough to come back for them.

Logan itself was a charming little mountain-valley town. But when I arrived at the construction site of our first Burger King, my excitement turned to frustration. The building was wrong from the ground up! They were using blueprints meant for Miami, Florida. Heated bathrooms? Not included—which meant frozen pipes were inevitable. There were even windows that couldn't withstand mountain weather. Worst of all, the broiler's exhaust vent was placed right against a wooden roof joist. That wasn't just poor design—it was a fire waiting to happen.

I called Burger King's Corporate immediately. Instead of thanking me for bringing the issues to their attention early, the brand-new Denver regional office took offense. They told me to get lost and stay out of their project. I was fuming. Malcom, the fiery Irishman, surprised me by cooling me down. "Patience, John. Let them finish."

When the restaurant neared completion, I came back with the punch list. Everything I had warned them about was now glaringly obvious. I refused to sign off until most of it was fixed. The only flaw left was the vent placement, which they forced me to accept. It infuriated me, but I had made my point.

Meanwhile, I was learning plenty from Mal on the financial side. At Walker Bank, the loan officers strutted in with a half-baked offer, with numbers that left us sorely wanting—especially given what we were bringing to the table. Once more, my NY temper almost got the best of me, but I watched as Mal sat at the end of the table, leaned back, and scratched his head as though confused. "Well, gentlemen, this doesn't make much sense. We said we'd leave about $35,000 a day in the bank account, and that affects something you people call yield, doesn't it?" The color drained from each of the loan officers' faces. Like a slap to the face, they were suddenly aware they weren't talking to a rookie. We walked out with a much better deal... and a solid, ongoing relationship with that bank.

I threw in ideas of my own for the restaurant, drawing from my grocery-store days. "If we buy inventory on thirty-day terms, that gives us a cushion of free cash. Less bank borrowing. Instead, we use vendor money, and it helps us grow faster." It wasn't normal operating procedure through BK franchisees, but Mal loved it.

Later, I refined the idea even further. The real crunch for any restaurant was from December to January. By March, sales always bounced back. I set aside just enough to bridge the gap and negotiated early-pay credits. Cash flow, I realized, was as important as profit. Larry Kessler had been right: the key to business was efficiency.

We opened the first Burger King in Logan in January 1977. I ditched my cast too early and ignored the throbbing pain. Bigger problem: nobody knew what and who Burger King was. Some customers confused us with Whataburger. Marketing only went so far; people had to taste the flame-broiled burgers for themselves. That first year, we barely broke even at half a million in sales, but the good news was that word-of-mouth *was* spreading.

I was tired of living alone in an apartment, missing my family. Once the business steadied, I bought a house in Logan and brought them out full-time. But I knew Logan wasn't the long-term growth vehicle, as it was too small a college town. The next site in Utah, Riverdale, felt right. In the fall of 1978, we opened with the highest volume in Burger King's Intermountain States history.

It seemed like we were experiencing overwhelming success, but it made me cautious. And even though I wasn't a control freak, if something wasn't working, I controlled the hell out of it until it did—and something was wrong here. I kept looking and looking, but the numbers in the books didn't add up. Compensating balances weren't showing where they should. Worse, one of our original partners doubled as our accountant, and his explanations were full of holes.

Within days, I hired my own CPA, Harlan Schmidt, and soon learned the truth: the other two partners were redirecting our Utah cash balances to open stores in Pittsburgh.

Not illegal, but definitely dirty.

I went to Mal. He was grateful I'd caught it. "Let's buy them out," he said.

We flew to Pittsburgh, laid out the facts, and confronted them. They denied wrongdoing and shot back, "If you don't like it, buy us out." Perfect. That's exactly what we planned.

Now with just Mal and me left, we opened our next store in Roy, Utah. We decided to try something new—a children's play area with a ball pit. Long before McDonald's started installing playgrounds, we were testing the idea. For one thing, we were in a family-saturated state. They bred like bunnies here, like Catholics. Family fun was a priority, and if you could have a burger *and* a ball pit for the rambunctious motley crew...? It seemed like a no-brainer.

At the Roy grand opening, I brought in Sesame Street characters to entertain the kids. It was a hit—until one woman marched up to scold me. "You shouldn't be doing this on Sunday. It's the Sabbath!" I gave her my best smile. "I'm Jewish. Yesterday was the Sabbath." She left flustered, and I was grinning the whole rest of the day, wondering when she would realize I'd had the characters there all weekend, anyway—including Saturday.

In 1978, I hired a new bookkeeper, Wendy, and kept abreast of what was happening in our growing empire. By 1979, Burger King was looking at opening a new restaurant location in St. George, Utah, a city that was about 90 percent Mormon. Because of that demographic, they wanted a Mormon operator. My Riverdale manager was both Mormon and an excellent employee, so I made him an offer. We had to prove $50,000 in the bank to start, so we parked it in the account long enough to get the letter from the bank and then immediately pulled the cash back out for our other growth needs. It worked perfectly.

That store in St. George also tested a new, two-broiler kitchen—one for dine-in, one for drive-thru. Trouble was, sales didn't justify staffing both. We turned the problem into a side business, renting the smaller broiler to other franchisees at their locations so they could test their grand openings. Another win-win-win, and no loss in cash.

Our next restaurant was in downtown Ogden, just five miles from my new home. It cut out the brutal winter commute over Sardine Canyon, and more importantly, gave me back family time. Logan had been beautiful, but Ogden was better for growth. Years later, my son Johnny would run that store and do a damn fine job.

With the St. George location now doing well, it was time to expand. Another town further north of St. George, Cedar City, had the benefit of the main freeway traffic thoroughfare and was a college town. Regarding Cedar City, I convinced Mal it was smarter to own the real estate than rent. We bought the land as well as the restaurant, which turned out to be one of the best moves we ever made.

About this time, the federal government gave us an unexpected gift. A new tax policy granted a 10% raw credit on payroll increases year over year. For businesses expanding like we were, the raw credit was rocket fuel. Essentially, Mal and I each got a $16,000 credit for *each store*. Between our multiple stores, all the personal income we made was completely sheltered—and while we had to claim it, it was sheltered from tax! Reagan eventually ended it with an alternative minimum tax legislation, but while it lasted, it gave us a foundation to become one of Utah's strongest employers.

Since Mal was primarily based in Wisconsin, even with his Vegas casino, he couldn't keep a close eye on the four Utah stores. This meant 95% of running all four stores was my responsibility. Since they were all going well, he introduced me to Larry Mialik, a retired All-American who had played pro football for a decade. Larry and I clicked, and together with Mal, we launched Southern Wisconsin Foods. Now I was helping run stores in Utah and Wisconsin. We bought a restaurant in Madison, right on the University of Wisconsin campus, and then developed another in Watertown.

Larry was the active partner on-site, with a district manager named Dick gaining ownership interest in Watertown. Later, Larry stepped back into a financial role, and together we spun off another company: Central Wisconsin Foods.

By then, my world had changed completely. I was no longer just managing Burger Kings for someone else—I was building them, financing them, and multiplying them with partners who thought as big as I did. I wasn't just a franchise manager anymore. I was a franchisee, learning lessons I'd carry for the rest of my life.

Lessons to Live By

I wasn't much of a student unless a subject lit me up, but business? That grabbed me. I learned to watch the players around me—their steps, their missteps—and realized life was about choosing who you wanted to dance with.

One chance came with Roger Staubach. Yes, *that* Roger—the Dallas Cowboy legend. He'd invested in Church's Fried Chicken in Utah, but the stores were losing money. He offered me a deal: take over operations, and if I turned them around, Mal and I could own them.

I understood the problems to know the solutions, but I was too new in Utah and too green with Burger King to take it on. I said no, but I never forgot how Roger treated me. Within five minutes, the Heisman trophy owner made me feel like an old friend. A great athlete, yes—but a greater man.

And Malcolm Kennedy? While he didn't hold Roger's fame, he had ethics, vision, and a partnership that continued to make great business sense. With him, I could grow at my own pace and was able to thrive.

The lesson? Trust your gut. Intuition is God's compass. You don't have to get along with everyone, but when it comes to partners—the people who shape your destiny—choose wisely.

"John confronts everything right up front; you know exactly where he stands about things. And that's one of the things I think I really like about him. He's not initially a warm and fuzzy kind of guy. You don't go up there and say, 'Give me a hug.' Yet behind that gruff exterior is a heart of a real gentle guy. He cares very deeply about the things he believes in, and he puts his money where his heart is."

– Tom Wheeler, Retired Business Owner, Pickleball Enthusiast

CHAPTER 10:

West Side of Buffalo to Western Cowboy

"The landscape of the American West has to be seen to be believed and has to be believed to be seen."
– N. Scott Momaday

All work and no play makes Jack—or John—a dull boy. If you think all I did during those years was crank out Burger Kings, I'll have to correct you. Moving West meant I'd landed in a giant playground, and I wasn't about to miss it.

In 1976, when we left Buffalo for Logan, Utah, I was more grateful than I can say. Buffalo produced 360 inches of snow that year—at sea level. Meanwhile, Utah was in a drought. The winter was so mild that the ski resorts never even opened. The next year, though, it snowed properly, and I had my first taste of Western powder. *What's this fluffy stuff?* I thought. Snow was supposed to be heavy and wet. It was a whole new world.

Almost immediately, the West tested me. Logan was expanding residentially, and I became friends with a developer named Steve

Saltern, who was building new homes near ours. He invited me to go horseback riding.

"Sure," I said, thinking it sounded like a great adventure. That Saturday, I showed up at his place in Mendon, cowboy hat and cowboy boots on, feeling pretty pleased with myself. Steve saddled up a horse for me, and we set off up the Wellsville Mountains.

For a Buffalo boy raised at sea level, looking 3,000 feet down from a narrow trail was unnerving, to say the least. I even pulled my right foot out of the stirrup. I figured, *if this horse goes down, I'm not going with it!*

We reached a small plateau near the top, around 12,000 feet, and dismounted for a break. Steve, who had been studying me for the last few miles, said, "John, you look nervous. You ever been on a horse before?"

"No," I admitted sheepishly, wishing he'd asked me earlier. "This is my very first trail ride."

Steve's eyes widened in shock and then narrowed. "I wish you'd told me sooner. This is the steepest vertical climb on the Wasatch Front. You've gotta be the dumbest S.O.B. alive to try this your first time on a horse!"

Well, guilty as charged. Still, I felt pretty macho, pretty invincible—until two girls came hiking up the same vertical climb on foot, faster than we'd been on horseback. That popped my balloon fast.

Despite the bruised ego, I was hooked. Horses fascinated me, and when he invited me on another, easier trail ride, I said yes.

Becoming a franchisee meant more than building a profile of successful restaurants; it meant time—time with my boys and my wife. For years, I'd been home only on weekends, *when I was lucky.* Driving 70,000 miles a year, I'd seen incredible places but wished my family could see them with me. I'd spent our early years of marriage trying damn hard to prove myself (especially to her folks), but by the time Christine and I were deep in raising kids, the proving shifted from me to *us*. Work, home, ballfields—it all blurred together, and I leaned in. Providing was how I showed love. Christine poured herself into our boys, and I poured myself into making sure she could.

If Christine had been able to have all the children she wanted, our lifestyles might have turned out differently. I'll never know. But fortunately, Christine had deeply honored my hard work and the long hours away, as well as the time we were together. And I appreciated the fact that early on, my wife, a beautifully skilled nurse, had come to the table and worked shifts for several months when I took that huge pay cut in the beginning. Once I could manage my own store and earn enough to support all of us, Christine was delighted to quit and stay at home raising the boys. And now, I felt she was living her dream.

As a partnership, we both wanted a better life for our own kids. I knew as a parent my voice got loud, and I held strong opinions, which I also loudly expressed during important discussions. To a kid, that could seem scary. Italians are known for being boisterous, and as the youngest of seven kids, if I wasn't vocal, I didn't get heard. But I wanted a deeper relationship with my boys than my birth father ever gave me—a more trusting relationship like the one Red gave me. Therefore, I coached Johnny's and Danny's baseball team, as well as Danny's soccer team.

If there was one place where life felt like pure joy, it was coaching my sons. No matter how long my workdays were, when I stepped onto a field with them, I felt ten feet tall. I wasn't just their dad—I was part of their team and could watch them grow, firsthand, instead of hearing about it from a phone call or a late-night play-by-play. I got to live their tragedies, lessons, and triumphs with them.

Some Saturdays it was baseball, others soccer. I was never the most skilled coach, but I was all heart. I taught them to hustle, to play fair, to shake the ref's hand even when he made a terrible call. The boys—my boys—gave me everything back. I can still see them in their uniforms, eyes bright with fire. I can still hear the laughter in the car rides home, grass stains on their knees, and ice cream dripping down their arms.

Christine was right there, too, cheering louder than any other mom in the stands. For those years when the boys were preteens and teens, we were in perfect rhythm: she handled the details, I was out on the field. Together, we poured everything we had into our sons. One thing I am most proud of is that my sons each thought I treated the other son better! To me, that meant I was doing my job as a parent.

As my Burger King career progressed, I once convinced my area manager to let me drive to a Florida conference so I could take everyone along—we made it a family trip to Disney World. That remained one of my sweetest memories—but it had been too short. While Chris had joined me once at a Burger King convention in Bermuda and another in Hawaii, those moments, too, had been so rare. Now, finally, I could build the life we'd dreamed of, outdoors with my boys and together as a family, and right away, I knew this would somehow include horses.

Steve kept taking me on rides, and I was hooked. I discovered horses read you better than you read them. Some were stubborn, some easy, but once I stopped spooking them, they accepted me without judgment. Before long, I bought my first horse—Corky Gil, a beautiful Appaloosa.

It was the start of a whole new chapter. Soon, I bought another horse, then two more favorites, Trader and Festus, so each of my sons could ride. I picked up a trailer and camper, and before long, we were riding and camping every weekend. Under the Milky Way, around the campfire, listening to my sons grow sleepy—it hit me that none of this could have happened back in Buffalo. We started riding on BLM land (Bureau of Land Management) until I bought a membership at La Plata, a club where we could camp and ride freely. It became our second home.

Family time mattered even more because each of us was struggling in our own way. Johnny, eleven and in middle school, faced prejudice for not being Mormon like most of his classmates were. Danny was quieter and younger. He absorbed some of his mother's homesickness and at times felt resentful. Chris missed her family deeply. In Buffalo, weekends were always spent with cousins and grandparents. Out here, she had to build a new life from scratch. She was strong, but I struggled when I saw her cry. I had to remind myself that if we'd stayed in Buffalo, the crime and urban decay would have eaten us alive. Utah wasn't perfect, but it was safe, hardworking, and full of possibilities for a hard worker like me.

Our new home on ten acres in Slaterville was flood-irrigated. I volunteered as ditch-master, learning fast that in the West, water is everything. I used every skill as a leader I had yet learned. In the meantime, I improved our existing barn with friends—six stalls with runs. We made new friends, too, and it seemed to me that Chris began to thrive. Vacations, outings, laughter—it warmed my heart to see her enjoy life again.

Then I bought a brood mare named Donna. I bred her, and soon my first colt was born—a palomino we named Celebration Bar. That was the spark. I bought an eight-stall barn with a tack room and a wash rack. Next, we built a large, indoor riding arena and put in a walker. I launched Crystal J Stables LLC and decided to race Celebration Bar. I hired a race trainer, Jerry Swanervelt, one of the best in the area.

At his first race in Pocatello, Idaho, Celebration Bar won! Standing in the winner's circle, I thought, *Wow, this is easy.*

Spoiler: it wasn't. He never won again.

I shifted gears, putting him into show training with Lawson Hadlock, a magician with horses, renowned as the very best. Celebration Bar started placing high—7th in Western Pleasure in the Intermountain Quarter Horse Association, 10th in English Pleasure. We showed him two or three times a month for over two years. My boys helped with everything—feeding, watering, and cleaning stalls. I made sure I worked just as hard alongside them. They learned tough lessons when pipes froze in winter, and they had to haul water in buckets three times a day.

I kept Celebration Bar as a stud. Between him, a paint stud named Pale Yellow, Johnny's horse Pepper, and two dozen brood mares, we had a full operation. I even installed a starting gate. With a full-time employee, we began training other people's horses too.

Not everyone appreciated it. One day, my mother came out from New York to visit. She found me mucking stalls and shook her head. "This is what you became successful for? To clean horse crap?"

"Mom," I said blatantly, "sometimes I work all day and don't know what I really accomplished. But when I clean a stall, I can see what I did. It relaxes me. It keeps me sane."

And it did. Horses were work, but they grounded me. With that in-house trainer, I took in outside horses and was able to help a lot of people. The operation generated just enough revenue in one year to justify the write-offs of the other six years of losses, which was more than most horse ventures could say. Most folks lose their shirts—and sometimes even their long johns—chasing horse dreams.

We even started the Allstars Junior Posse, giving kids—including mine—the chance to sharpen horsemanship skills while they made solid friendships. With Burger King and other sponsors, we outfitted them in custom blankets and rode in the Ogden Pioneer Days Parade, performing in the rodeo five nights straight. Johnny was able to do some extraordinary work with horses that lasted into his young adulthood. One thing was certain, it built his confidence, his ability to do hard things, and his work ethic.

Although, as time went on, Chris and I personally discovered that sometimes the horses were just too much work. Since I had an employee covering the chores, I bought a cabin in the mountains and a houseboat on Lake Powell to balance out the ranch life with family fun.

Eventually, when raising horses became more work than joy, I sold the property, barns, and equipment to a veterinarian. Amazingly, I got back every dollar I'd invested. People said, "That never happens in the horse world!" but it sure did with me.

A friend of mine, Karen Wisner, had her own explanation. "John, you don't have lucky stars," she said. "You've got a golden horseshoe up your ass. Everything you touch turns out gold."

That wasn't exactly true. But maybe... close.

Lessons to Live By

The six years I spent with the horse adventure could've looked like a loss on paper—but in reality, it was anything but. Financially, it sheltered my taxes, and I walked away with every penny I ever invested. Even better, when I bought the extra five acres, the owner lived in an ancient log cabin and asked to stay for one more year. When she moved out, I knocked the old place down. Here's the kicker: I had put 80% of the purchase cost into that cabin, and when I destroyed it, the tax code allowed me to write it off as a loss. That's a strange but true business lesson: sometimes tearing down the old makes way for something far more valuable.

But the best payoffs weren't financial at all. Johnny, back from college in Montana, worked with Lawson Hadlock, a legendary trainer, and discovered a knack for breaking horses. He loved it, at least until he realized that backbreaking work doesn't always make for a lifelong career. Yet those years gave us something priceless: conversations about life, love, business, and money, all made easier while mucking stalls or working with a skittish colt.

Johnny remembers starting even earlier, at thirteen, helping me open our first Burger King. He still quotes me:

> "If you wake up in the morning and say, 'What a good-looking son of a bitch I am,' you're gonna fail. But if you look in the mirror and say, 'All right, asshole, what'd you screw up yesterday, and how can you improve today?' then you'll succeed."

Not exactly poetry—but it stuck. Deciding horses weren't his long-term career choice, he came to work for me, opening Burger Kings and helping build and remodel them so efficiently, it took my breath away.

My son Daniel, on the other hand, thrived in academia. He once told me, "Having to clean stalls every day and manage my time made college easier." Danny went on to college at the University of Wisconsin, graduated in three years on the Dean's list and Phi

Beta Kappa honor society, continuing on with two master's degrees and then a doctoral program—all on scholarship. He would never make the kind of money Johnny would make, but I was very proud of him for his own talents, skills, and contributions to education and community.

Two very different sons, two very different paths—same stable beginnings. I would always tell myself, *If both of them were happy, and neither of them ended up on Prozac, I'll have done my job.* Every moment spent with them and every dollar spent on horses was worth it—golden horseshoe or not.

Beyond family, the horses opened doors into our community. We sponsored the All-Stars Junior Posse—an amateur horse-riding group. The All Stars got involved in parades and local events, where I found clever ways to merge business with service. When Burger King switched from Coke to Pepsi, I had custom-made Pepsi hats for our customers and gave some to our Posse. Suddenly, our community relations program got national recognition. BK Corp already required us to put 4% of sales into branding and marketing, but I personally always added another 2% locally. That came from what I learned at Tops Markets: grow your community, and your community grows you.

I'll pose this question: How much do you spend with Amazon? And how much do they spend giving back to your town? If you own a business, remember this: community involvement is its own competitive edge. Maybe the guy across town sells a better burger—but he can't say he's feeding firefighters, sponsoring kids, or bringing Whoppers straight to the firehouse between calls.

For me, giving back was never a chore—it was a thrill. Community service lit me up. It tied my business, my family, and my purpose into one whole. It reminded me that, as Helen Keller once said, *"The best and most beautiful things in life cannot be seen, not touched, but felt in the heart."*

That's the real lesson to live by.

"In my business, there's so often people who are blowing smoke. And you never really know what you've got until you walk on site; wherein I know if John says, 'I'm gonna take care of this, I'm gonna handle it…' I could just forget about it and I know it's gonna be taken care of."

– Randy Merrill, Talent Buyer

CHAPTER 11:

Building a Burger King Dynasty

"A new dynasty is never founded without a struggle. Blood makes good manure."
– Emile Zola

Life has a way of making sure you get all the lessons. If you brush by something the first time or refuse to learn a deeply-needed lesson, it will come back around to haunt you until you get it right... or break it completely. Either way, you'll learn some great lessons. This happened often in business. *That* I could solve, get around, and fix. When it happened in my personal life, it was tougher.

My first horse, Corky, started going lame. I couldn't bring myself to put him down. Instead, we went for a last, short trail ride, and I left him with a group of wranglers in the mountains where he could live out the short remainder of his days in the peace of being alive, enjoying nature and its nurturing.

Still, when I got the call that Corky had died, I cried like a baby. I sobbed and sobbed and couldn't stop. What I didn't realize was that I wasn't just experiencing the loss of Corky, but all the grief I'd held in for so many years after Chris and I lost our first babies—the twin girls that never had the chance to grow up with us. I hadn't shown my wife my grief because I was taught to be "strong." In my culture, I was supposed to come across as a tough S.O.B. During crises, I wanted to be the stalwart one, always holding it together. I was very soft-hearted, but had only broken down and sobbed in private, as I thought my role was to push forward, to bury the soft spots, to be the steady rock Christine and the boys needed. I didn't realize my silence was costing us more than my words ever could.

As the boys grew older, our family's rhythm stifled. They didn't need me as much on the game field or the court, and Christine's focus began to change. One night in St. George, the crack in our marriage finally split wide open.

She looked at me across the elegant resort room, her voice low but steady:

"It's great here. I'm known as Christine—not the 'Burger Queen'," she said sarcastically, "not the wife of 'the Burger King'."

"Why would you say that?" I asked, flummoxed and defensive. At this point, I'd built about 20 Burger Kings. It's why we could even be here at this luxurious spa, with its saunas and pools and massages in the first place.

"I don't have an identity," she said softly. "I don't know who *I* am."

I froze, unsure what to say. Then she added, sharper this time, "All I know is that I no longer want to be known just as your wife. I want to know who I am."

Her words still echo in me years later. They cut deeper than anything I'd ever faced on a field or in business. I wanted to argue, to defend myself, to remind her of everything I'd sacrificed, we'd sacrificed, every late night, every dollar earned. But that wasn't what she wanted. She didn't want proof. She wanted *me*.

And I didn't know how to give her that.

So, I went back to work… on the business, but not on our marriage. Again, it was because I simply didn't know how.

I continued building restaurants. Southwestern Foods wasn't slowing down—if anything, it was running faster than we could chase it. To handle the flood of paperwork, payroll, and constant fires to put out, Mal and I put together K&G Management Services. It wasn't glamorous, just a shared office, a way to split overhead, and a system to keep things from grinding to a halt. But sometimes the unglamorous decisions are the ones that save your neck. That one kept the wheels turning while we chased new opportunities.

One of those opportunities took us to Wisconsin Rapids. We sent Terry Miller, one of my sharp young Utah operators, to run the store. Terry had the gift of seeing around corners, the kind of manager you could trust to put out a fire before you even smelled smoke. At first, it looked like we'd nailed it. Expenses were under control, marketing was clever, and promotions were drawing crowds. Then the bottom fell out.

Sales didn't just dip; they collapsed—sixty percent gone almost overnight. We hadn't changed a thing. The burgers were still hot, the fries were golden, the staff was friendly. So why were customers vanishing?

The answer came in thirty-foot letters, towering over the streets:

Don't eat at Burger King — they use non-union labor!

The words glared down at you from every corner. It didn't matter if you were on your way to church or the grocery store—you couldn't drive across town without being told you were crossing a picket line by ordering a Whopper.

The kicker? It wasn't true. But truth doesn't carry much weight when you're sitting in traffic staring at a thirty-foot lie.

Mal jumped into action. His NFLPA background gave him credibility with labor folks, and he sat down with union leaders to hash it out. He showed them our employee manual, pointed out that our pay and benefits stacked up better than some union contracts. That's when they admitted our store wasn't the target. Corporate was. But knowing you're collateral damage doesn't help much when your register is bleeding out.

I was furious. I booked a flight to Miami, marched into Burger King's corporate headquarters, straight into the CFO's office, and dropped the store keys right on his desk.

"You run it," I snapped. "This ain't our problem."

He looked at me like I'd gone off the rails. Maybe I had. But I wasn't about to let their fight take me down without swinging back. That led to a shouting match that probably had the walls shaking in downtown Miami. I wasn't there to be polite—I was there to make them feel the heat of what we were taking on for their brand. After rounds of back-and-forth, they finally conceded a little rent relief. It wasn't enough to make us whole, but it was enough to stop the bleeding.

We tried again in Stevens Point, putting Dick in charge. For a while, it looked good. Then it didn't. Dick developed… let's call them extracurricular habits. He didn't run things the way we did, and I was too busy in Utah to notice the cracks until they were canyons. By then, it was too late. Lawyers got involved. When the dust settled, Dick walked away with Watertown, and we kept the rest. It stung, but Southwestern Foods survived.

Then came the biggest blow of all.

In 1984, Malcom passed away. Mal wasn't just my partner—he was a storm, a spark, a force of nature. He was brash, loud, brilliant, sometimes reckless, often impossible, but never boring. I had loved being his partner and learning day in and day out. The NFL ring Mal wore wasn't just jewelry—it was proof. Proof that he'd been on the field in a different sort of way than the players, taken his own hits, and come out as a champion. He wore it like a badge of honor, and it carried weight in every room he was in. He wasn't perfect, but he could walk into a room full of people who didn't trust him and walk out with a handshake deal no one else could have landed. He'd see disaster, grin, and say, "We can make this work." And somehow, we did. Without him, business didn't feel the same. Without him, I didn't feel the same.

Just when I thought I'd survived the worst, fate struck again. The Logan Burger King—my very first—burned to the ground. As it turns out, it was the same cursed vent problem I'd been warning about since 1975! Wood joist, heat vent, disaster waiting to happen...

It happened.

I'll never forget standing there in the night air, smoke thick in my lungs, watching flames lick through the roof. People had warned me that in business, you had to be ready for anything. But no one tells you what it feels like to watch your very first dream go up in flames.

Fortunately, no one was hurt. But the loss still hit like a fist to the chest.

My son Johnny had started working with me at our new Ogden, Utah, store, doing a fantastic job. He learned fast like his old man, and I found he had remarkable business sense. We didn't always agree on everything, but we always, always worked it out. I found that a lot of his ideas balanced mine, and it felt great to have a guy on my team again that I could trust.

I brought Johnny in on the rebuild of the BK across the street from the burned-out site. Only this time, I made sure every shortcut was ripped out of the blueprint. If I was going to put my name on a building again, it was going to stand. If a vent even looked at a joist the wrong way, it got moved. Watching that first store burn tightened something in me. Buildings can disappear in an evening; the only thing that lasts is the people you build and the reputation you earn when the lights go out and the smoke clears.

That was one of a hundred reasons I got pulled deeper into Burger King politics. A bunch of us in the Rockies formed the Intermountain Franchisee Association—Utah, Idaho, Colorado—so we could stop acting like lone prairie towns and start acting like a territory: the power of local-store marketing and distribution *together*, buying power *together*. Northern California had a version, Southern California had one, and pretty soon other regions copied the model. It was simple: if we wanted to survive corporate weather and regional storms, we were better off linked arm-in-arm.

I was elected to the board. At first, I thought it meant I would have influence. Then I realized the truth: the board had votes but no teeth. It was more ceremony than power.

Then came 1988, and with it, massive change. Grand Metropolitan of England bought Pillsbury—and with it, Burger King. Overnight, a British company was calling the shots. Franchisees across the country realized we needed a louder voice, so we pulled together and created the National Franchisee Association (NFA).

A year in, I stepped down and became Director of Franchise Relations instead. That was real work—representing franchisees in lawsuits, negotiating settlements, hashing out policies with Corporate, and helping mom-and-pop operators survive the rollercoaster of the fast-food business.

One of my closest allies in that fight was Rick Cowley, who led the Southwest region. Rick was sharp, passionate, and had vision. He once said, "John was a giver. He gave his time, his resources, his know-how—helping the local operator with better marketing or operations, then turning around and helping Corporate at a global scale. I learned a great deal by watching John do what John did." I never thought of myself that way, but Rick meant it. Together, we reshaped the NFA into what he proudly called "an association of associations" and that's exactly what it became: a coalition that could speak softly to one another and loudly to the mothership when it mattered.

Somewhere in there, I got tapped to help run our National Annual Convention. Thousands of franchisees, heavy corporate presence, one big stage. That year, Burger King's development director was a sharp Brit named David Fitzjohn. My job was to work *with* him but also make sure franchisees' rights and needs didn't get flattened. I decided to do what I did best when the tension gets thick: use comedy like a crowbar.

I walked out in a black suit and tie, slicked-back hair, full mafia swagger, and laid on the accent as I did back in the day with Jaycees, but this was a whole new crowd. "You know, da association wanted me t' represent dem and deal wit dis new guy," I said, scanning the room until I spotted him dramatically. "I tink his name is... David... Fitztoilet."

The place detonated. Franchisees roared. Execs howled. And Fitzjohn himself? He was guffawing, a good sport all the way. I told the crowd I had video evidence of how David and I had made a pact to work together, then rolled a scene from *A Fish Called Wanda*—John Cleese hanging upside down outside a building while Kevin Kline holds his ankles, Cleese pleading, "All right, all right, I apologize. I'm really, really sorry. I apologize unreservedly." The roof of our convention almost came off! From that moment, the ice was gone. We weren't adversaries—we were partners. Humor had bridged the gap.

Grand Metropolitan had its own ideas about "real work." They rolled out something called the Entity Franchise. In theory, it was a great innovation: you didn't need a big-money operating partner anymore; you could have a managing director responsible for operations while investors financed growth. That freed strong operators to scale—back your best people, build more restaurants, and move fast.

But then came the part they didn't understand. Thinking they were just licensing a brand, they eliminated over 1,500 operations people from the system—the field support that helped ensure franchisees stayed on spec, solved problems, and kept standards tight. To me, that was like cutting the rigging off a ship mid-storm.

Long term, I believe, those decisions really hurt the brand. Yet in the short term, that Entity structure opened the door for me to do some unconventional things, like buying out Hardee's units later on to rebrand into BKs. In 1996, when the Utah Hardee's franchise was going out of business and forty units were on the block, I bought eleven in northern Utah and one in St. George. My son Johnny worked his guts out as we remodeled or rebuilt all twelve in nine months flat! Because of him and his team, we earned a development award for adding twelve new restaurants. It was true: blessings, curses, and opportunities have a way of showing up together... wearing the same hat. It's what you do with them that counts.

I hadn't built a full-service restaurant in a while because the math could get ugly. Land, building, and FF&E (furniture, fixtures, and equipment) had crept toward $1.5 million—a *long* way from the $170,000 FF&E only back in Logan! My appetite for that kind of risk had cooled. Then, around 2003, at the national convention, the company rolled out a kiosk concept for high-traffic locations. That's when my mind lit up.

"In southern Utah," I told them, "we've got Zion National Park—over a million visitors a year for at least seven months.[7] Let's put a Burger King in a gas station."

Blank stares. No one had married a major QSR brand with a C-store like that—ever. But the building was already there, the parking was there, and ninety percent of the utilities were already paid for. "And you do understand," I added, "gas stations don't make their money on gas. That's why they all have a C-store. This could be a win for everybody."

To my delight, Burger King gave me a "provisional okay" to explore it.

I drove down to Hurricane, Utah, twenty miles on the highway in and out of Zion and sat with the owner of a Chevron station. I pitched him plain and simple: "When you're a tourist, getting ready to drive into or out of Zion's Park and see a Burger King, you'll stop for fresh food—not a tired corn dog on rollers. While they eat, we'll ask if we can top off their gas."

I also promised I wouldn't serve BK dessert items, so his C-store kept the sweets. And I offered a clean lease: $2,500 base rent per month or 8.5% of sales—no triple net on gas, electricity, water, insurance, property tax, outside maintenance, or bathrooms. He was already paying ninety percent of that anyway. I used the Entity Franchise structure for the first time, raised $100,000 from investors, and took a 5% interest with full operational control.

To keep what that means simple: that little "gas-station Burger King" netted $100,000 in year one. Corporate had granted me a one-year provisional franchise as a test; after those results, they granted a five-year deal with three five-year extensions.

That's when Burger King started sending other franchisees to see what I was doing. After the fourth or fifth tour, I realized I was doing

7 https://www.nationalparked.com/zion/visitation-statistics.

their job for free. So, I drew a line. "I'll share precisely how I sell the lease and operating agreements," I told visiting operators, "but there's a $10,000 fee." Since my contracts were under Utah law, they could take the templates to their own counsel to state-proof them. It saved them tens of thousands of dollars and months of guesswork. Over the next few years, I opened nine C-store restaurants in Utah and Wisconsin. Once people saw a Whopper next to windshield wiper fluid and Slim Jims, they stopped asking if it could work.

From the time of my fourth store, I'd learned that even when the restaurant is profitable, the *real* money is in the dirt beneath it. You couldn't own your real estate with McDonald's, but you could with Burger King. If you leased, in twenty years, you were staring down another twenty-year lease at whatever price *the market* demanded—whether the location was tired or not. If you owned, you controlled your rent, and you could depreciate the property. The business paid the mortgage; time and IRS rules did the rest.

After we bought out the Hardee's stores in Utah, I met Karl Malone of the Utah Jazz—two-time NBA MVP, broad as a barn door and twice as friendly. He came in to shoot a commercial for Burger King at my West Roy restaurant. Between takes, he kept talking about wanting to get into the restaurant business, so I offered him a chance as a financial partner in Preston, Idaho. We formed MVP Restaurants. He was an investor, not a franchisee. That's when Burger King called and asked me to put him on as franchisee for public relations purposes.

The night before the Preston opening, a member of Karl's staff told me his marketing rep thought I was taking advantage of Karl's name. I pulled Karl aside at the opening. "This restaurant is a pimple on my ass and a pimple on your ass. For me, this is a fan's way to say 'thanks.' I don't need your money. Yes, we use everything we can to promote each location, but I'm not taking the wrong kind of advantage. I want the store to win." Karl read the room, shrugged with that easy grin, and we got on with it. He was a good guy, and later he invested in our Price, Utah, restaurant as well.

That opening day in Preston, the school district closed early and bused the kids to the store. Karl gave a motivational talk—big guy, bigger heart—and watching those kids look up at him, you could feel the energy in the room lift.

Afterwards, he asked me, "You want to ride to Jackson Hole?"

"That sounds great... but I've never been on a bike."

"I'll take care of that," he said.

Next thing I know, my son Johnny and I are taking lessons from Karl's security guard—who also happened to be a Salt Lake City motorcycle cop. He met us by the Utah State Fairgrounds and taught us how to ride a bike at five miles per hour. "Any idiot can ride fast," he said. "At speed, the physics help you. Slow is where you learn control."

After mastering those drills, I rode to Jackson Hole with Karl and six other bikers. We stopped in Preston to tip our caps at the gas-station restaurant, then cruised two-lane back roads at fifty miles per hour. Dropping into Star Valley, the pine scent hit me like a tonic. I felt more awake than I had in years.

In Jackson, Karl asked, "You ever run a river?"

"Yeah, once. Loved it. You?"

He shook his head. So, the next day we ran the Snake, Karl up front—no surprise there—which made balancing the raft a little more interesting than usual. Snowmelt had made the water high and fast. We hit the first wave, and he yelled, "I think we need more training!"

I laughed all the way to the take-out.

Between the motorcycle cop's lessons and that river, the hook was set. I was addicted to cross-country travel on a motorcycle. I bought a Harley Road King—customized, of course—and headed straight for Sturgis for their famous annual motorcycle rally of tens of thousands of hard-wired bikers. My new buddy Dick Weber brought his brand-spanking-new Fat Boy. When he fired it up, another friend's wife Jackie Wilson and I said in unison, "Sounds like a Honda!" Then came the moment we realized that while in Sturgis, Dick's bike required its 500-mile oil change–necessary for the life of that motorcycle. While it sat on the rack, we "helped" by spending

$4,000 of his money on upgrades—starting with pipes so it finally sounded like a Harley. We laughed the whole time.

That trip hooked me. Summers became measured in miles: Utah's Highway 12, Telluride, Going-to-the-Sun, Banff, and the Beartooth Highway at 11,000 feet—switchbacks so breathtaking you felt you could touch the sky.

Best souvenir? A leather Harley jacket made for Karl's MVP seasons. It fits, it's heavy with memories, and it's one of my treasures.

I never took it for granted that becoming a franchisee made this life possible. I had a safe home under the Wasatch, time with my boys in the outdoors, and the freedom to take one big bike trip a year to remind myself there's a world beyond spreadsheets. But none of it was handed to me. I worked my ass off to earn every mile.

As an operator, I ran tight ships, but I rarely owned more than five to ten percent of a given unit. When someone had the desire to invest with me, I learned to take a percentage of sales off the top—before profit—as a management fee. And when it came time to sell, our agreement stipulated that the management fee stream had to be bought out before profits were distributed. That way, I captured the value I'd built in the operating system, not just the ebb and flow of a P&L.

Along the way, we bought into several gas stations with their owners—equity in the dirt and the pumps, not just the burger counter. Johnny turned out to be a hell of a designer and builder. I was proud of him. I formed Diverse Management to handle the BK properties we owned and to consult; my son took the president's chair and ran with it.

Perhaps that was one of the greatest benefits of all.

Lessons to Live By

In the stress of all the building—bringing on partners, letting go of partners—I discovered you need two things to survive: humor and a thick skin. Malcolm had both. He loved a good argument, and I gave him as much hell as he gave me. Half the time, we ended up doubled over, laughing.

In his personal life, he was a heavy drinker. Then one day, he quit cold turkey. I admired him for that. What I didn't admire was his newfound mission to get *me* to quit something—my weight. I told him, "There's nothing worse than a born-again anything." Didn't stop him from ribbing me.

The irony? The man loved Snickers. He'd swear them off, and I'd sneak one onto his shoulder or the backrest of his car. He couldn't resist. The best Snickers in the world are frozen Snickers, and since he lived in Wisconsin, I sent him a case of 250 mini frozen ones one year. You can imagine the profanity that poured through my phone line. But I guarantee you this—he didn't throw them away.

Humor aside, business is where the biggest lessons came. Every Burger King had to deal with "Ideal Food Cost." I built my own spreadsheets in Excel to track the gap between ideal and actual. That's how I learned accrual accounting. My brother, for all the grief he gave me, was right about one thing: "If you ever want to sell something, you've got to show a profit."

I also learned the art of creative-but-legal deductions. Government rules said you couldn't expense your daily commute, but if you went anywhere else, it counted. Since I traveled constantly between Utah and Arizona, I always logged mileage. I even expensed my motorhome trips to southern Utah—because technically, I *was* visiting a store. My CPA finally shrugged and said, "The IRS has to accept it."

Here's the truth about business: it all involves risk. You will make mistakes. You cannot let that stop you. The trick is "risk management"—taking calculated leaps instead of blind ones. My advice?

- Do your homework.
- Trust your instincts.
- Trust your God.
- Then, take the plunge.

Because that plunge into entrepreneurship could be the best decision you ever make! You'll meet characters—some wonderful, like Malcolm and Rick, and some you'd never want to cross paths with again. But no matter what, you'll grow as your legacy grows. And if I've left anything behind, I hope it's more than the burgers and the buildings. I hope it's the friendships and the heart.

"John ran for the school board. And he came to me because I do some political work with people; it's part of what I do. And he said, 'I want to run for the School Board. What do you think?' I told him, 'I pity the Ogden school board. You're going to win, and you're going to stir things up.' And he did."
– Robert Bell, Owner of Bell Printing

CHAPTER 12:

When Light Pierces the Darkness

"Every time your heart is broken, a doorway cracks open to a world full of new beginnings, new opportunities."
– Patti Roberts

If I could go back, I would have listened—really listened to my wife, Chris. But I didn't know how. And the silence grew until it swallowed us whole. After twenty-two years, our marriage ended. I made sure she was provided for, but money can't buy back closeness. It was grief all over again—and I was still experiencing grief that I didn't know how to name or share.

Years later, when I stood by Chris' hospital bed, I finally understood. I listened. She forgave. For a moment, we were us again. But it was too late to rewrite the story we had lost.

What I learned was this: I could coach my boys on every field in Utah, I could coach new businesses to life, but I failed to coach myself in the most important skill of all—listening to the woman who loved me.

While I was married to Christine, I was driven. When the marriage fell apart, however, I was still driven—only this time, I was driven to drink. It wasn't good.

One night, I found myself in a Salt Lake City hotel bar, alone with another half-empty glass, staring at a row of equally unhappy faces. That's when a scene from *Saturday Night Fever* flashed through my mind—John Travolta muttering, "This ain't no freakin' life."

That's how it hit me. This wasn't life. It was a crutch. The glamor was gone. And right there, I quit alcohol.

But quitting the bottle didn't stop the emotional spiral. Without Chris, and with the kids being off on their own, what was I working for? Then, as my marriage disintegrated and I was terribly distracted, I got another punch in the gut—betrayal.

Wendy, my office manager and bookkeeper since 1978—the one I trusted to keep the wheels turning—came to me with her head down.

"I've been taking money from the company."

I just stared at her. *What? Embezzling?*

She admitted her husband was a drug addict. What started as "a little here, a little there" had become tens of thousands. Cold shot through my entire body as I looked at her. It was bad enough that she had done this to me, especially when she knew what I was in the middle of with my divorce, but I came to find out that the only reason she told me was that the IRS had scheduled a full compliance audit.

Irony number one: if not for the audit, I might never have known. Irony number two: I passed that audit clean—except for her crime against me. In a strange twist, the IRS would eventually ask me to give a keynote speech at their offices in Ogden, Utah. "I'm probably the only businessperson in your history who will thank you for an audit," I told them, "because it saved my business." Their faces were priceless.

But in the meantime, I was facing the deep pain in my heart of the betrayal and the damage in the business. I told the local police investigator, Detective Lucas, "I can't believe this. I brought her in part-time to help her get her degree, then brought her on full-time in the early 80s. Only this year did I discover she was stealing—because of that audit."

He nodded and kept writing down details. I couldn't help it. Anger and deep sadness were reflected in the tears I held back and the fire now coursing through my body that had long replaced the cold.

"I can't believe she did this to me," I said to Lucas. "She's in my will."

"This involved drugs," he said pointedly. "You're lucky it didn't get that far."

When Wendy was sentenced, I visited her before she was led away to serve years in prison. I looked at the woman I had hired part-time so she could go to college and earn her degree. I looked at the woman who I hired full-time after she graduated. And I looked at my heart, which was breaking. I had to turn to God in this moment, even though I didn't understand much about Him.

"I can't help you if I don't forgive you," I said. "And if I don't forgive you, I can't be forgiven for my own issues and sins." I knew I had plenty, so right there in that courthouse, I let it all go. I took one last look at her and said, "I forgive you." And I left, with her sobbing.

But forgiving myself was harder. I had lost Mal to death, Chris to an ongoing divorce, and nearly my company to embezzlement. I was emotionally broken, financially strained, and deeply alone.

One Sunday morning in 1986, it all came crashing down. I tried calling everyone I knew, but of course—it was Utah, and everyone was at church.

"Note to self," I thought later, "never have a nervous breakdown on a Sunday in Utah!" With no one to reach, I drove myself to the hospital and checked into the psychiatric ward.

They drugged me and left me in a haze, which only made me feel worse. Thankfully, my CPA and friend, Harlan Schmidt, tracked me down after hearing a desperate message I'd left. He came to my bedside and said, "Do you want to pray with me?"

I nodded. Only it wasn't the rote "Our Father" or "Hail Mary" from my Catholic childhood, but a prayer from the heart. His words were raw, real, and full of love. It steadied me in a way the medicine never could.

Still searching, I went to see the priest at the local Catholic parish. I hoped for comfort. Instead, I got questions, judgment, and the same fear-of-God I'd grown up with. I left feeling emptier than before.

Harlan invited me to his home to listen to two young Mormon missionaries. At first, I was skeptical—I thought their tears during a lesson were theatrics. Then I realized it was the Spirit moving them. That shook me. For the first time, I wondered if maybe God was closer than I thought.

I didn't convert right away, but I did start praying. A lot. My neighbor, Orville Holly, a seminary teacher, welcomed me into his classes. He was honest, even about hard topics like plural marriage, and he taught me to wrestle openly with faith rather than hide from it.

Slowly, my prayers softened me. I was gentler with my sons, more tender with my friends, more aware of people's pain. I was still carrying grief—but for the first time, I felt God walking with me.

Eventually, I decided to join the Church of Jesus Christ of Latter-day Saints. When the LDS missionaries told me that too much time had passed and I'd have to take the Gospel lessons again, I shook my head. "No way. We'll do all four lessons *this week*." And we did.

Hugging my mother after my baptism, I whispered, "Now you've been here both times I've been born." I meant it. I felt completely light and free, and she could see that the tears in my eyes were real and genuine joy. Hers matched mine, for me.

Johnny also saw the change. Years later, my son told me, "I don't need to join a church. You raised me right. But I'll say this: you're a much better person now than you were before you joined."

That meant the world.

My first calling in the Church was teaching the young men in our congregation. In addition to the manual, I tossed in my life lessons. I even bribed them with Burger King. If they remembered the previous week's lesson, they got a free Whopper card. Nothing motivates a teenager like food.

And it worked. A young man once asked in class, "Is it true Brother Gullo will be forgiven for all the stuff he did before baptism?" I cut in before the bishop could answer: "You can't just 'cop a plea' in this church. But do you really want to gamble that you'll live long enough to change? Don't wait." Later, that same boy asked me to speak at his missionary farewell. That floored me.

God had started to change me. One night, I prayed harder than ever before, pouring out my heart for change, for light.

The very next morning, I opened my window and saw my pasture fence covered in balloons and a sign: *Brother Gullo, we love you!* A teacher over the youngest children's classes, "Primary," later told me she'd been praying and felt God tell her to get the kids involved in making it. She obeyed, and it became one of the most miraculous, tender mercies of my life.

During this season, I met a wonderful woman named Karen. At first, we were simply friends, both a little cautious, both carrying our own scars. But friendship deepened into something steady and strong for a time. As our budding romance developed, we began going to church together, and two years after my divorce from Chris, Karen and I decided to marry. At first, we had a civil marriage performed by the ward bishop. Twelve years later, we were sealed in the LDS temple.

Not long after, I lost my mother. She had carried a Catholic guilt that never left her, convinced that her divorce had barred her from heaven. Watching her go to her grave, afraid of God, broke me. I wept, not only for her loss but for the centuries of fear that had been laid on her shoulders. In that grief, my conviction crystallized: God is not a punisher. He is love, mercy, and second chances.

Then came my father, Red. He was tough as nails, but the bottle owned him. After Mom died, he sank into a guilt-filled depression he couldn't shake. One day, I said, "Dad, would you let me give you a priesthood blessing?" I expected him to scoff, but instead he said yes. I laid my hands on his head and prayed for peace, for healing, for release.

The next day, he showed up at my house, pool bag in hand, grinning like a boy on summer break. He was lighter, freer, as though decades of weight had fallen from his shoulders overnight. For the short time he had left, he lived differently—more himself than I'd seen in years.

It felt like God had reached down and touched him. And in that moment, I knew—if God could heal Red, He could heal anyone. And my heart wrapped around the light.

Rejuvenated, I went back to building full-service restaurants. In 1993, we opened in Layton, Utah—a big opening. In 1994, we bought four Burger Kings from the company in Wisconsin. My original franchise, Northwest Foods Limited (NFL), ended up opening eleven restaurants, selling three, and closing and rebuilding another in Roy when we put in that ball pit I'd pioneered earlier.

I formed BWR Restaurants in northern Utah with investors—ten percent ownership for me, zero liability on the debt or leases for me. Beautiful structure.

In the meantime, my extended family remained vital in my world. I kept in touch with my surviving sisters, even though most of them, except Terri, had been incredibly upset that I had moved Mom and Red out to Utah, especially because when my parents sold their house years prior, I told them to keep their money and to do what they wanted with it. Why? I remembered all those years of Mom working such long, long hours to support us all. I'd wanted to support her and Red in the way they once supported me–especially the only one left at home when they married. Mom had her very first car all to herself when she'd come out here, and she and Red never had to work another day for the rest of their lives. I knew Mom and Red had been very happy here in Utah, and very well cared for. That to me was most important.

When Terri and I had talked about it, I'd told her, "One of the problems is, when you're successful, in your estate planning you leave things to the people who come after you. I want to do something for the people who got us here." She agreed.

My sister Rose was in Florida, where she'd moved with her new husband Andy, who was somewhat well off. When my sister Joanne became a widow, she sent her son to go to school near me at Weber State. However, she got upset that I put him to work, just like I had my own sons. I never believed in free rides. Still, knowing how important wheels were to success for a young person, I cosigned a car for him so he could get to work and school and back. Joanne was still irritated.

When my sister Terri's second husband died, she needed a new start. I'd never let go of the fact of just how brilliant she was. I invited her to come to work for me.

"I need to step away from work, and you need to get busy building things," I suggested. She agreed, and I was delighted to give her ten percent ownership in the company. I was right; she was brilliant and brought in further success with her dynamic point of view. We didn't always agree on decisions, but we respected the hell out of each other.

Then I faced a surprising irony: my older brother Jim wanted to move from Florida to Utah. He saw my success in Burger King and wanted me to hook *him* up this time.

I was a little taken aback on the inside. But I quickly said yes and formed a corporation with the name "New Start" in St. George. Some friends of mine thought I'd lost it after what Jim had done to me—firing me from his restaurant business in New York, right in front of Red all those years ago. He'd known it would crush my young family and me.

Even Johnny knew the whole story of all that Jim had done to me because I'd shared it openly with him—and Johnny thought the idea of giving this opportunity to Jim was a *baaad* idea.

Still, despite what my friends and other family members thought, I knew it was right to forgive him. I carried the Jaycee Creed inside me, and I heard the words in my mind and heart that I sought to embody every single damn day of my life: "*...that the brotherhood of man transcends the sovereignty of nations; that economic justice can best be won by free men through free enterprise... that earth's* *great treasure lies in human personality; and that service to humanity is the best work of life."*

I pondered those words and thought, *No matter what he's done to me, I can choose to represent that higher brotherhood. I can give economic justice, even when it was not granted to me. I can tap into my treasure of human personality and be of service to him and his family.*

Through the years, I'd remained stubborn about helping family. Plus, to be honest, I had a quiet agenda. I wanted to prove to my big brother that I wasn't the guy he'd told my father I was. Plus, I really did want the best for him and his second wife.

Maybe, I thought, *the Utah spirit will rub off on him.* Still, I knew not to trust him further than I could throw his spreadsheets. New Start opened another restaurant a year and a half later.

Jim would come to me for advice on everything. He'd run a bar before and had someone run a couple of restaurants for him after me, but you can't run 14 fast food restaurants effectively with that knowledge alone. He was a businessman, not an operations guy, so he never left the office. I spent time in every store, no matter how busy I was, and tried to share what to do differently so he could be successful.

Helping my brother was a huge risk. As I signed the paperwork, I didn't shake, but I knew it could turn out well or it could turn out in disaster. Only time would tell what Jim would choose to do with the gift.

In total in my career, I would build, own, and operate fifty Burger Kings across three states, with many extraordinary partners.

By 1999, however, I was ready to put my efforts and money towards other things. After nearly three decades, I started selling. First Wisconsin, then Arizona, then central Utah, then southern Utah—holding back the four I'd already sold to Johnny. He carried them very well for a time, until he finally sold those last four himself in 2018.

Looking back, I see a pattern: build the thing, then build the structure that lets the thing survive you. K&G kept my project with Mal growing instead of buckling at the knees. The Intermountain Association kept franchisees from getting picked off one by one by Corporate politics. The National Franchisee Association gave voice to the people who wore the aprons and paid the franchise fees. The Entity structure—as flawed as Corporate had made it—let us try new business structures, like C-stores at Zion's front door. Real estate gave us ballast. The fees I took off the top paid for the brains of the operation. And relationships: Mal, Rick, Terry, David, Karl, Johnny, turned near-disasters into new, abundant chapters.

I didn't set out to be a leader. I set out to make the next right decision, and then the next one after that. But somewhere along the way, people started looking over at me when fires broke out, and I started the habit of being the one who stood up when no one else was.

If there's a secret to all of it, it's not brilliance. It's stubbornness with a sense of humor. It's knowing when to throw the keys on a CFO's desk and figuring out how to sell a Whopper next to wiper fluid the next. It's telling a Hall of Famer his restaurant is a pimple on your ass—and meaning it kindly. It's riding into Star Valley at fifty miles an hour with your son on the next bike and realizing you are, against all odds, exactly where you're supposed to be.

Fires, billboards, lawsuits, losses, wins. Fifty stores. Nine C-stations. One leather jacket. One son, successfully running what we built. I didn't do it alone. I never did. But I showed up, and when I got knocked down, I stood back up. Every time.

And in the end, that's the whole playbook of success.

Lessons to Live By

I believe in Jesus Christ, that He is the Son of God. I believe he came here to give us a second chance to be with Heavenly Father forever. It's a good thing he is a redeemer, because there has been a lot I've needed to be redeemed from!

Mormonism was a tool that greatly worked for me at a time when I needed it. I will never forget the love of God, and I do my best to never take the love of others for me for granted. It was a beautiful steppingstone to a greater spiritual life of service. Like Red taught me, "Judge not, lest ye be judged," I don't care what religion or faith anyone has. If their beliefs make them a good person and they treat me and others right, that's all I care about. My father's simple lesson, although crude, is the way I still live my life. "Don't shit on nobody and don't let nobody shit on you."

In fact, I have many Jewish friends, and I share with them in humor, "I feel so sorry for you! You're still waiting for the Savior, so you can't repent yet." They just laugh, then razz me for my beliefs. **The beautiful part is that love remains in the room, with mutual respect inherent for all.**

And as far as laughter? Wisdom came to me from Cid Caesar: "It takes the same amount of energy to cry as it does to laugh, the choice is yours. Always choose laughter."

Not everyone in my family found love. I sure had my struggles with it. But I'm delighted that both of my sons seem to have chosen wisely. They've found their perfect partners. That gives me hope for the generations coming after.

For years, I've gathered my grandkids together in little family meetings. I wanted to pass on not just the funny stories, but the hard-earned lessons too, so maybe, just maybe, they wouldn't stumble in the same places I did. You could call it my own brand of insurance policy.

Here's one of my "grandpa-isms" I passed along: if something's stealing your peace day after day, don't ignore it. Either roll up your sleeves and fix it, or find the courage to walk away. Don't let life's biggest relationships—or your own mistakes—chew holes in your joy.

Because here's the truth: people say I have a passion for living. And I do. But the fire in my belly has always come from my kids, grandkids, and great-grandkids. That's what life's about. That's what makes the ride worthwhile. At this point in my life, I count it as my greatest blessing of all—to be alive long enough to know four generations of Gullos.

Now that, my friends, is passion worth keeping.

"John was somebody who saw a vision and was willing to put his money and time and effort and everything else behind it. I liked that personality, because it was cool to see things happened... You need somebody to come in there and shake it up a little bit. And John came in and definitely shook it up."

– Trent Christofferson, Financial Planner

PART III
Spirituality & Service

"If you can dream it, you can do it."
– Walt Disney

CHAPTER 13:

From Gullo to Geppetto – a Footprint

"What you leave behind is not what is engraved in stone monuments, but what is woven into the lives of others."
– Pericles

One morning in the bathroom as I was trimming my mustache, I looked into my reflection. The words of a Michael Jackson song filled my head. The lyrics from "Man in the Mirror" kept echoing in my head: *"If you want to make the world a better place, take a look at yourself and make a change."*

And that's exactly what I'd been doing—changing. Letting God truly into my life. Letting love in, too. Those choices had turned me into a different man. And with change came the question that had started gnawing at me:

What about my legacy?

By then, Johnny and Danny were married, and grandkids were filling my world with laughter and perspective. Just like their fathers had once transformed my life, these little ones were reshaping me all over again. I knew great-grandkids wouldn't be far behind.

Johnny had come home from his year at college and married shortly after—it was the best decision he ever made. I watched him blossom into a savvy businessman, uncanny in both detail and big-picture vision. He could zero in like a hawk one moment, then soar like an eagle the next. Working with him in business often took my breath away.

That didn't mean we always agreed. John and Johnny. Two stubborn, type-A, no-nonsense New Yorkers in one office? Our debates could shake the walls, rattling the rafters like lions roaring on the savanna.

Once, Jeri—Johnny's wife—had popped into our main office to visit during one of those knock-down-drag-outs. She looked at us, frazzled, as we suddenly switched gears, joking about where to take the family to dinner.

Jeri's eyes were wide with disbelief.

"Wh-what? How can you two fight like *that*... and then just go to dinner?"

Johnny and I grinned. We knew the truth: business was business, family was family. No business deal was ever worth losing each other.

Danny, on the other hand, carved his own path in academia. He started at the University of Wisconsin, paying out-of-state tuition that nearly gave me a heart attack—over $40,000 a year. But he pulled off the impossible: graduated in three years, Dean's List, Phi Beta Kappa. From there, he collected scholarships like baseball cards—earning a Master's in History from the University of Toronto, a second Master's in Theology from St. John's in Wisconsin, and eventually a doctorate in history from the University of Chicago. Watching him rise through academia filled me with pride.

All of this stirred deep ponderings inside of me. I hadn't had much guidance myself. Goodness knows my birth father—their biological grandfather—was never around for me. I wanted to be different than that man. In fact, it wasn't until long after he died that I found out from my mother that he liked to make things with wood. In high school, I remember I had picked Wood Shop willy-nilly, because it sounded like fun. We didn't build much, but one time my class made a podium for Mr. Fallon, our English teacher. It started as a prank–nobody liked him. But when we presented it, he was so touched, he broke down in tears.

I learned a few profound lessons that day. First, you get more with kindness than you ever will with sarcasm. The lesson hit deeper than the grade I got—though the A-minus was nice, too. Second, people are touched when you build them something. And third, apparently they could be as well when you wrote something.

For example, I'd once written a poem that had won Mr. Fallon over:

To men, women are such troublesome things,
Through them they give the things they cherish:
Money, love and old school rings.
But these are not lost or left to perish!
For women repay them by doing housework
That breaks their backs,
These acts are not lost or forgotten
Men repay them by for their acts,
Buying minks and diamond rings.
– John Gullo

Mr. Fallon loved it, but years later I realized how much of that poem was rooted in false beliefs I'd carried into marriage and beyond. Remembering all of this, I had a profound realization: it all comes down to love. Showing it. Sharing it. Living it.

So how could I share my love with my kids and grandkids, when I wasn't really taught how to show it?

Suddenly, a deep desire for them came into my mind: In their plastic, throw-away world, wouldn't it be something if they could point to something lasting and say, "My grandpa made that."

That thought turned me from Gullo into "Geppetto."

The first thing I built was a simple Tic-Tac-Toe block set. The grandkids loved it. Then, with more tools at my disposal, I started building bigger things: a six-foot-tall rowboat-shaped bookshelf for my new wife, Karen's knick-knacks, complete with a corner dock to display it. Then, a handmade, old-fashioned clock for her. And for little Jordan, my first granddaughter, a dollhouse.

That one nearly broke me. I'd foolishly made it out of particle board—it was so heavy it became a burden. One Christmas, I noticed a plastic Barbie house inside their home, and outside, discarded, sat the wooden one I'd built. My heart sank. I loaded it back into my truck. Mistake or not, it became a fixture for years for other granddaughters when they came over.

Lesson learned. After that, I built smarter: doll cradles, desks, wall-mounted dressers, shelves for Kylie, a towering display for Jordan's mountain of Beanie Babies. Johnny even let me build the fireplace mantle and a massive wall bookcase in his new home that he kept for decades.

I reveled in these years. I always wanted my grandchildren to feel at home in my presence. My wife Karen and I truly enjoyed spending time with our grandchildren from our earlier marriages. We sought to make them feel at home with us, regardless of who came from who. For a couple of decades, we were great partners in nurturing them, taking time with them at the cabin and snowmobiling, as well as traveling with them throughout the world, and giving them keepsakes that might last.

Eventually, though, my attention deficit disorder and logistics caught up to me. When I sold that home, I moved the woodworking shop to a warehouse I had bought to store business equipment. But being 30–40 minutes away, I rarely used it. My passion fizzled, especially when I saw some of the pieces I'd worked hardest on that didn't make it into my grandkids' adult homes.

Famous author Stephen Covey once said, "The need to leave a legacy is our spiritual need to have a sense of meaning, purpose, personal congruence, and contribution." I agreed, and one day, I made a different kind of legacy decision. I donated the entire shop—tools, wood, supplies—to Youth Impact, an inner-city program teaching kids woodworking. And so, from Gullo to Geppetto, my footprint became less about the objects I left behind, and more about the love—and the lessons—woven into my family, and now into the lives of children I'd never even met.

That sparked something bigger... but I had no idea just *how big* it would become.

Lessons to Live By

The moral of the story is that the joy of giving is the best thing. Creating anything is worthwhile, whether it is appreciated or not. To this day, my greatest joy has been in giving. It's my love language. I also found a tremendous benefit in teaching my grandsons these lessons. When I worked with them one-on-one, like Red worked with me, I was able to tell stories, to set an example. These were the things that lasted, even when the things I built for them did not.

Your job is to leave a legacy. You never know who will receive it or how they will receive it, but leave one anyway. I've learned how to celebrate the wins along the way. For nearly forty years, each time I went to my son Johnny's house, the fireplace mantle and the large bookcase I built for him brought warmth to my heart.

In his recent remodel, it's been replaced, but I learned that legacies aren't written in marble—they're carved into the hearts of the people you love.

"Speaking of personal character, John is a man with a heart of gold, a man who, if he agrees in a cause, or a belief, or some kind of change, he seeks for the betterment as a whole. John's integrity is foremost; if he tells you something, he's going to abide by that."

– Scott Conley, former Police Incident Commander

CHAPTER 14:

Making American Dreams Come True

"Everybody can be great because everybody can serve."
– Martin Luther King, Jr.

In 2000, I started the American Dream Foundation—ADF for short. My big idea? To finally give Ogden the kind of 4th of July celebration it deserved. Can you believe the city hadn't celebrated our nation's birthday in over thirty years? Not a single firework. Not a sparkler. Nada. Utah's Pioneer Day on July 24th got plenty of love, but the 4th of July was treated like a banished cousin. That didn't sit right with me. A patriotic fire was lit under me to show the kids of Ogden—especially those in the inner city—what it felt like to gather and celebrate America together.

Meanwhile, my son Johnny was working like a madman running his businesses, and playing just as hard. He and his wife, Jeri, had thrown themselves into demolition derbies. I'm not kidding. They strapped themselves into old junkers and slammed them into other cars—for fun! They weren't just in it for the laughs either; they were competitive and tough, and most of the time they were the ones doing the pummeling. Jeri would climb out of her car grinning like a Cheshire prizefighter. It was hard not to laugh and shake my head. Work hard, play hard, get pummeled hard—that was their motto.

But here's the thing about Johnny: his mind never rests. Hobbies have a funny way of becoming businesses. Before long, he wasn't just picking up debris and driving in more derbies—he was organizing them! I loved seeing his passion, and the crowds? They came out in droves. Four, five thousand people, packed into stands just to watch cars smash into each other like angry bumper cars on steroids. There was camaraderie, cheering, celebration, fundraising for nonprofits, and, of course, beer. He was catering to the hearts and minds of blue-collar families, and they loved it. When I stood in the middle of one of his events, surrounded by the roar of engines and the equally loud cheering of fans, I couldn't believe it. People paid good money for this kind of chaos.

That gave me an idea. What if we paired this kind of crowd-pulling spectacle with something bigger, something that celebrated the country we loved while raising money for Northern Utah charities? Johnny and I sat down, two stubborn minds crackling with possibility, and decided to make it happen. We decided we'd put on the 4th of July event—massive fireworks, a demolition derby, and eventually even more—that cost taxpayers *nothing*. Year by year, we'd grow it, make it bolder, and funnel the profits into the community.

Now, one thing you should know about Johnny and me—we don't do well being told how to use our creative energy. Politics and power struggles always felt like chains around the ankles. For a time, I served on the Ogden City School Board. I saw there how good intentions to help kids and education too often got strangled by ego and bureaucracy. It drove me crazy, trying to get anything effective done. The bright side was meeting Don Belnap, who became a lifelong friend. He served with me, shared my frustrations, but used to shake his head and say, "John's got an admiral's mind and a sailor's mouth." He wasn't wrong. As much fun as the two of us had working together, let's just say patience for red tape was never my strong suit.

So, when it came to the 4th, we decided we'd win without asking permission. I went straight to Mayor Godfrey, whom I liked and admired, and laid it out.

"Here's the plan: fireworks, a beer garden, a demolition derby, and more to come."

He blinked. "What do you want the city to do?"

"Nothing," I told him. He stared at me as if I'd just sprouted antlers.

I explained, "When I lived in New York, the citizens—not the government—ran celebrations like this. It was an event *by the people, for the people.* We're going to do that here. All I need is the city to cover police, paramedics, and fire crews in case the fireworks misbehave. Beyond that? Stay out of the way."

I could tell he didn't know whether to laugh or call security. But I meant it. That was the point. Johnny and I knew if the city got too involved, we'd be stuck in meetings and strangled by politics instead of making magic happen. We needed to run this event like a business—tight, efficient, and accountable.

Plenty of people said we were crazy: "Too risky," they called it. "Too expensive." But I remembered Tom Brokaw's words: "It's easy to make a buck. It's a lot tougher to make a difference." We had set out to make a difference.

We signed up a bank and a credit union as our first big sponsors, rented the Ogden City Arena, and by 2001, Hot Rock'n 4th was born.

Johnny and I were deliberate in our strategy. Concessions, we knew, were the bread and butter of any event. So, we brought in small vendors, hauled in an extra broiler from Burger King, and snagged a beer license. We tapped nonprofits for volunteers and paid their charities for every hour worked. And to keep the peace, we invited Ogden's police force: any officer who showed up in uniform got free admission for himself and his entire family. That guaranteed plenty of blue shirts wandering the grounds.

When people asked about my biggest fear, I answered honestly: "Either nobody shows up—or too many show up."

Turns out, it was the latter. More than 6,000 people poured in that first year. Burger King literally ran out of food. Vendors scrambled to resupply. The place buzzed with life. It was exhilarating.

Afterward, I gave the city a full report: what worked, what didn't, and how we'd improve. They couldn't tell us what to do—and we liked it that way—but they respected our accountability. That was always my mantra: in leadership, there are positive mistakes and negative mistakes. Positive mistakes sting, but you make changes going forward. Negative mistakes are the ones you repeat without learning anything from them. In philanthropy, like in business, I vowed we'd only make positive mistakes.

The second year, we doubled down. Nearly 10,000 people came. We sold mountains of food, rivers of beer, and kept ticket prices low—all while donating to charity and building ADF's reserves. Friends at Burger King, like Rick Cowley, shook their heads. They couldn't believe how far we'd come.

My wife Karen participated in some of the planning, and for several years during Hot Rock'n 4th, there she was, with her sleeves rolled up, working with her friend at the concessions stand to benefit *Prevent Child Abuse, Utah.*

By year three, America First Credit Union stepped up as a $10,000 Presidential Sponsor. Their request? Make our event more family-friendly. So, we fenced in Lorin Farr Park, right next to the arena, and transformed it into a wonderland. We brought in inflatables, magicians, kids' games, a train that wound through the park, and even a classic car show.

One of the benefits was that we could sell beer throughout the entire facility. In Utah, the only way you can sell beer is by creating a special place for beer-only sales. The Derby stadium didn't have a problem, and by fencing in the park, we didn't have a problem with state law. As I recall being told to me by the beer supplier, over the years, we broke Weber County's single-event draft beer consumption record three times, averaging 44 kegs of beer between 1:00 and 9:00 p.m. on the day of the 4th. Not bad for Utah.

With the number of officers around and the scorching summer heat, folks stayed merry but not messy. Thousands of beers, and not one fight or disturbance due to respect for the police and their families. I call that risk prevention at its finest.

We kept adding flair. Monster trucks thundered in for two years (until the expense of liability insurance drove those particular trucks out). So, we brought in a monster truck ride for kids—an instant hit. We added a dirt bike course with soaring jumps, then rock crawlers grinding their way around the arena. By year three, we were drawing over 15,000 people.

And of course, fireworks were non-negotiable. I wanted a $20,000 show—with a twist. We dazzled the crowd with a spectacular "grand finale" at twelve minutes, then, just when everyone thought it was over, lit up the sky for another eight. The crowd went wild. I stood under those explosions, patriotic music booming, children squealing with delight, and looked at Johnny and my grandkids with tears in my eyes. Two businessmen pulling off something the city hadn't dared—and winning without permission. That was the American Dream.

We also had to think about fire safety. Twice, dry brush near the arena ignited, and thank heaven the fire department was on hand. We needed them as much as the police.

When the event outgrew the arena, we moved to the Weber County Fairgrounds. The derby was still the star, but we added open-air concerts. I'll never forget the thrill of bringing in Collin Raye, then Diamond Rio. We even introduced rodeo events by building portable starting gates at our own expense. Tickets covered it all—derby, rodeo, concert—one all-American package.

Then came the Freedom Rally. Once Karl Malone had gotten me hooked on riding a Harley, charity bike rides became a passion. Why not roll it into Hot Rock'n 4th? With the help of Joe Timmons, the local Harley-Davidson owner, we gathered over 1,000 bikers every year. Riders got commemorative pins when they signed up, wearing them proudly during scenic parades through downtown Ogden, escorted by the highway patrol.

One of my greatest memories was leading riders over the North Ogden Pass. Cresting the summit, I paused and looked back. A river of motorcycles snaked all the way to the top of the mountain. It took my breath away. To be the leader of that parade was unforgettable. The ride raised thousands for charity, and years later, when Hot Rock'n 4th eventually ended, I gifted the rally to the Children's Justice Center so it could continue fueling their mission.

We couldn't have pulled any of it off without incredible partners—Scott and Debbie Conley, Jim and Jacque Wilson, Dana and Cheryl Morvello. They gave heart and soul.

ABC4 even sponsored us for two years, broadcasting live from the park! One year, they branded a demolition car, and my daughter-in-law Jeri drove it like a warrior. She battled to the end and took second place. I don't think I've ever been prouder of watching her behind that wheel.

Over the years, Hot Rock'n 4th became more than an event. It was a force. With 750 volunteers from thirty-three charities, we raised three-quarters of a million dollars. It was a magnet for tourism, a source of pride, and proof that when private citizens come together, nothing is impossible.

Mike Leatham, our consultant on memorabilia pins and shirts for these events, summed it up best: "I see John involved with lots of charities, and people get him involved. But he also tries to get them to do their own jobs. He doesn't just give without expecting people to elevate. He pushes everyone to rise higher."

Eventually, though, the winds shifted. An accident on an inflatable ride, new insurance demands, and a mayor who didn't share our vision forced us to stop. I kept waiting for someone else to pick it up, but no one ever did.

Still, for nearly a decade and a half, Johnny, our partners, and I pulled off something unforgettable: a patriotic celebration, of the people, by the people, and for the people. It lit an admirable fire in our community. Hot Rock'n 4th will always be at the heart of what the American Dream Foundation stood for: ordinary men and women doing extraordinary things with nothing more than determination, creativity, and love for their country. Still, even though my hands were tied on certain ends, it didn't stop Johnny's and my energy to make a continual difference. Besides, now we had contacts and connections with the best people in the world—service-oriented people are, after all, in police, nonprofits, fire districts, school districts, and for-profit organizations all across the Wasatch Front. When a need arose, we were there.

The American Dream Foundation went on to do many, many, many more projects.

Knowing how I had grown up on the edge like a lot of kids in Ogden, latchkey, single moms doing what they can, I believed they needed something that researchers at universities would discover later: when one young person has one adult person in their lives who *believes* in them and supports their dreams and talents emotionally, they can create a stable life. I set about making sure that the people in the community could be those believers, who already worked with street kids, and could have the funding and resources to reach as many as possible. I liked motivating other people to see the beauty in these organizations, and I made fundraising videos so they could help themselves to grow.

I thought about what influenced me most as a hot-headed teenager besides Red, and it was music. So, I got musicians to work with the police to develop music CDs with the kids' kind of music but uplifting lyrics that they would still think was "cool" or "sick" and would listen to.

Every project spurred another, and another, and another. I loved the ones that gave kids a chance, that taught them about America's beginnings and that any one of them could grow up to be President, like the Children's Treehouse Museum where we not only set about helping them secure more funding, but also did an entire, permanent program called the Great American Freedom Trail, which included a replica of the U.S. Presidential Oval Office, the president's desk and all. All 5th graders in Ogden visited on a field trip as part of their schooling. We funded a replica of the Printing Press of the

Declaration of Independence, for each kid to print and sign with a quill pen and all, right under John Hancock's name.

While at the Presidential Desk, each student signed legislation as if he or she were President of the United States! I wanted them to visualize leadership in their future, and that any one of them could become president—because that's just how great the opportunity in America is.

I was so on fire about patriotism for America, it colored everything I did in my nonprofit and every step I took. One song we produced was called "Hymn to America" with Lex D'Azevedo, the extremely talented, former producer of the *Sonny and Cher* show. I made sure it got into schools and nonprofits and churches and restaurants across the Wasatch Front.

Then, a couple of passion projects brought everything from my childhood and young adulthood full circle. The first was a part of honoring the past. Working in conjunction on multiple projects for multiple fire agencies, we realized a great need and created an *American Fallen Fire Memorial,* a monument for fallen firefighters lost in action. Similar to a war memorial, the families of the fallen appreciated this deeply, as nothing like it was created anywhere that was so honoring, visitable, and felt sacred to their loved ones, and included their names etched in the marble. I was also able to honor Red and made a full tribute to him as a part of it.

The second was about helping to secure a happy and beautiful future for young adults with Down syndrome. I could never forget the young people in Niagara Falls who had so literally changed my life, from inward-focused to outward-focused, and who brought such joy to their communities every day just by being alive. We gave them the ability to learn a trade, help others, and be in a like-hearted, uplifting community while they did it.

I agree with Anne Frank when she says, "How wonderful it is that nobody need wait a single moment before starting to improve the world." These decades of projects, "of the people, by the people, and for the people," sparked a flame that could never be extinguished. In fact, it just got us started!

Take a look at a few of the projects that American Dream Foundation, and eventually the John Gullo Foundation, played a role in:

1. Served on the board of Enable Industries, a nonprofit teaching life skills and a trade to individuals with disabilities and those with Down syndrome. There, we designed, built, and funded a dining room for clients with Down Syndrome right in their warehouse, so they could enjoy community with each other while still learning and earning a living.
2. Donated a new warehouse to Enable Industries—named the Rose Robinette Building in honor of my mother—to enable them to earn contracts for shredding paperwork for large clients like the IRS.
3. Donated funds to get the first Youth Futures event started, providing emergency shelter, temporary residence, and supportive services for runaway, homeless, unaccompanied, and at-risk youth ages 12–18. Johnny later assisted by getting them heavily discounted kitchen equipment through Burger King suppliers, so that more funding could go towards programs.
4. Funded and worked with Prevent Child Abuse to produce a fundraising CD and video that created awareness regarding child abuse. We shared offices with them for five years, covering their expenses. We chaired their annual fundraiser for one year and participated in several. We also sponsored keynote speaker Thurl Bailey at one gala.
5. Produced a fundraising video for the Children's Justice Center, which served abused children, then produced and handed over The Freedom Rally, a motorcycle event to continue raising much-needed funds for this endeavor.
6. Provided relief efforts to the Red Cross in the aftermath of Hurricane Katrina. We were later honored at their gala for our efforts.

7. Funded Youth Impact Classrooms with four computers and printers.

8. We sponsored Youth Impact "Youth in Transition" for the naming rights of their building expansion. In addition, we produced a fundraising video and were active in an American History event for the kids, and provided a timeshare in Cabo, Mexico, for gala fundraisers for three years. We also provided equipment for Pickleball to be added to activities.

9. In honor of my sister, we funded the Terri Wells Study Hall at ATC Applied Technology College.

10. Provided funding for the American Fallen Fire Memorial in Ogden, with a gorgeous ten-foot bronze statue of a firefighter, entitled "EveryDay Heroes." It was a tribute to my father, Red Robinette, and his 30 years on the job and hundreds of names etched into the marble of the exhibit, in honor of these heroes.

11. Funded the James F. Robinette Fire Prevention Fund. This program taught fire safety in 16 Ogden area elementary schools, in support of the Ogden Fire Department's Boots & Bunkers Program.

12. Provided pickleball paddles, balls, and portable nets to establish Pickleball in the Ogden School District, even supplying paddles with school logos on them.

13. Sponsored the book *Apollo* in both Weber and Ogden School Districts, and purchased the book written by Barry Asmus, for the Ogden and Weber School District 6th-grade classes. It taught finance and how the free enterprise system works at a 6th-grade level.

14. Donated a handicap vehicle to Weber School District—a single father with eight children, one of whom is paraplegic, won the vehicle for his family in a fundraiser. He said it was life-changing for them. (I was so touched when the family came to pick up the

vehicle and were so well-behaved, they didn't fight over seats. I told my director, "Let's do something for them for Christmas!" Only I didn't realize they were Seventh-day Adventists.)

15. Funded Ogden City Police Department's Let's Play Program for five years, providing after-school activities for inner-city kids. We also sponsored their Gang Prevention Program, producing the album *Red Sky* on CD, featuring good rap music with excellent messages. We also sponsored the officers' Hello Programs at Junior Highs, with the rap singers performing and each kid getting a copy, plus extra copies for officers to give to kids while on patrol. Donated Funds to the Police Benevolent Fund for many years. Additionally, we produced a recruitment rap video with Thurl Bailey to encourage kids to become cops.

16. Produced patriotic videos, such as "Hymn to America," "Song to America," "Stand Up," "In the Company of Heroes," "My Responsibility to America," and more to be used in schools, programs, and museums.

17. Produced fundraising video for The Children's Treehouse Museum. Funded the Great American Freedom Trail, which included a replica of the Oval Office that all 5th graders in Ogden could visit as part of their curriculum. Each student could sit at the desk, and sign legislation, imagining themselves as the President of the United States. It was a great way for kids to visualize themselves as future leaders. We also funded a replica of the Printing Press of the Declaration of Independence. Each kid had the opportunity to print and sign one with a quill pen, under John Hancock's name.

18. Funded a pontoon fishing boat for American Heroes, as part of their homeward bound initiatives to overcome PTSD and reenter society.

19. Funded the Indeed Playground at the Christmas House Box facility in Ogden for abused kids. Also ran a fundraiser for them,

An Evening of Christmas Giving, with a concert at the Raptors' ballpark.

20. Sponsored keynote Mark Mathabane, a speaker and human rights activist who grew up in South Africa during Apartheid. He spoke at an assembly for Ogden and Weber School Districts, held at Weber State University.
21. Provided funding for Alpine Wyoming Pickleball Courts to get the health craze started in a notoriously sedentary area for older adults and young kids.
22. Provided funding for custom pickleball paddles for Star Valley Pickleball groups to sell and raise funds for further development of pickleball in Wyoming.
23. Funded Dolly Parton's Imagination Library as a free book club for kids in the program for three years running in Ogden.
24. Funded Crescent Moon, the art program that teaches local native children how to paint and draw. We funded the teacher in the first year and continue to support the program.
25. Funded videos, publicity, website assistance, and more to the Statue of Responsibility Foundation, to bring education to hundreds of thousands and more about the importance of both liberty and responsibility in our civic responsibility—and inspire a new generation.
26. Donated a fire truck to Bombardiers for Los Barriles in Mexico.
27. Donated half the funds to purchase the first and only ambulance for East Cape Health Center, Los Barriles, Mexico.
28. Made a significant donation and participated in group volunteer labor to enable a children's home in Cardonal, Mexico, to be built in 2024. This facility was meant to provide temporary housing, education, and nurturing for children with family members un-

dergoing treatment for cancer and other diseases. Also donated a portion of the annual operating cost for three years.

29. Funded a trailer and remodeling for a roving Pickleball Hall of Fame, for the purpose of continuing to educate the public about the history of pickleball, as well as the players and leaders who turned the sport from a little-known hobby to a worldwide phenomenon. While the trailer proved unfeasible, plans go forward for a permanent display in the future.

And the list continues to grow...

Lessons to Live By

Mahatma Gandhi once said, *"The best way to find yourself is to lose yourself in the service of others."* I'd add this: if you want to become larger than life, serve somebody. If you want to get past your own fears and insecurities, serve somebody. And if you want to cut through red tape and build something extraordinary, serve with people whose hearts beat the same as yours.

I won't pretend my nonprofit work was purely altruistic—oh, hell no. But I learned that service could create a win-win. Instead of pouring money into government taxes, where the results don't often circle back, Johnny and I poured resources into our community. The return? Richer lives, healthier communities, and a front-row seat to collaboration and celebration. Did I enjoy major tax benefits for myself and my family? Oh yeah, I'm no dummy. But even that pales in comparison to all the things we were able to do for our community.

The best part was bringing the family along. My son Johnny and I became closer through philanthropy than we'd ever been. At my 20th leap-year birthday celebration, he said, "What my grandfather Red instilled in him, he instilled in me... we are here for a short period, and we enjoy giving back." Johnny and I may not agree on everything, but we always agree on love, family, and service. That's legacy.

Service doesn't always start with fireworks—it starts small. A handshake. A bookcase. A soccer team. A wall in a children's home that needs painting. You never know what will come of it, but you show up anyway.

And sometimes, you've got to risk big in service of others. Johnny and I never knew which projects would fly and which would fizzle. From programs for individuals with Down Syndrome to patriotic celebrations, from coaching kids to championing first responders, we had no guarantees. But we dreamed big, we acted fast, and we stayed the course—even when others didn't show up. That's how miracles sneak in the door.

Because here's the truth:

- **Service isn't a title, a position, or a trophy.**
- **Service is the soil where miracles grow.**

Want to be extraordinary? Want to see miracles? Look left. Look right.

Then, step across the street and help.

"Grandpa let me work with the American Dream Foundation for a long time before I was a full-time worker as a teenager. Then, as soon as I started college, he had me work for what I was going to have, but they provided for me in a way to learn and to grow. So, he always supported me: college, serving an LDS mission, marriage, becoming a mother—he's been there every step of the way. He expected me to work for it. He always gave opportunities to work hard and earn money. He treated me, Dalton, Kaitlin, and Tyson all the same."

– Jordan Martin, granddaughter

CHAPTER 15:

Harmony Over Discord – It's Not All Black & White

"Prejudice is a burden that confuses the past, threatens the future, and renders the present inaccessible."
– Maya Angelou

Our nation has seen division before, but lately, it feels like the volume's been cranked up. The gaps between people, especially the ones between race, culture, and politics, have become wide enough to swallow whole friendships and destroy entire families. We have become overwhelmed by our vast differences. Yet when I stand next to my buddy Thurl Bailey—6'11", former NBA star, musician, keynote, and humanitarian—I'm reminded of something the world still needs more of: a *real* conversation about love.

Thurl and I met the way most lifelong friendships don't: I "won" him. True story! At a silent auction benefitting kids, he offered to teach a basketball clinic for 15 children. I won and brought 150 kids! Fortunately, he didn't blink. He poured himself into those kids like they were his own, and by the end of the day, neither of us was the same. Turns out, the man who once towered over NBA courts can make a gym full of kids feel like champions—and make a stubborn old businessman rethink what it means to lead, love, and show up.

And oh, yeah… if you haven't seen the dynamic "Big T" in person or on the court during his tenure with the Utah Jazz and Minnesota Timberwolves, I'll let you in on a secret: Thurl Bailey is not only Black, but also famous for being a Rockstar—on and off the courts!

As we became fast friends, we realized we were two men from two very different worlds—different colors, different decades, different paths—and yet, somehow, parallel lives. What we learned isn't just a story about us. It's a story about what still holds people together during a divided time: mentors, accountability, faith, and the choice to see each other through the lens of love. As Mother Teresa said so profoundly, "In this life we cannot always do great things. But we can do small things with great love."

How do we do that? We show great love by starting conversations with people different than ourselves. By sharing our stories. And realizing that both our similarities and our incredible differences can help bring the world together. Below is a spirited conversation my co-author and I had with Thurl Bailey, filled with hard-won wisdom and shared with Thurl's permission.

THURL:

> "I was born in D.C. in the middle of the Civil Rights era. My parents had clawed their way out of North Carolina, trading tobacco fields for the grit of Prince George's County, MD. Gangs, drugs, prejudice—it was a battlefield for a Black kid. But it was also a proving ground, and Mom, Retha, had a rule: no 'average' grades. 'You're Black,' she'd tell us. 'The world's already stacked against you. You don't get to coast. You're going to make a difference.' She and Dad attended Martin Luther King's rallies and his 'I have a dream' speech. And while Dad taught us resilience and strength, Mom taught us fire and passion. They weren't perfect, but they drilled into us that no one hands you a future—you build it."

JOHN:

"As you read already, Buffalo, New York, wasn't a cakewalk, either. Our neighborhood was dubbed 'the Slums,' this pie chart of Italians, Irish, Poles, Jews, and African-Americans, where you stayed in your slice after dark. Organized crime strutted like royalty, and unfortunately, my older brother Jim bought their version of the American Dream wholesale. It was Red, my stepdad, who kept me from going the same way. Red came late but saved me early. He taught me to work, to lead, and to steer clear of quick-money traps. Without Red, I'd have been running with the wrong crew instead of building something real."

THURL:

"Who knows where I might have ended up? I always had a penchant for leadership and service, but I was crushed when I got cut from my junior high basketball team *twice*, by a coach who only saw what I was: a tall, clumsy kid with no skills. Then along came Coach Cole. He didn't care that I was raw. He took me aside and said, 'I see potential in you that you don't even see. Commit, and I'll be here an hour before and after every practice.'

Those extra hours? They built me. He didn't just make me a ballplayer; he taught me how to grind when nobody's watching, and how to hold myself accountable even when it hurt, and how to lead without crushing spirits.

As I became more skilled with so much practice, Coach Cole ran interference in his additional 'spare time' to prep me for scholarships, which enabled me to play for and attend NC State. Coach Cole taught me what leadership really looks like: seeing what could be, not just what is."

JOHN:

"I didn't have scholarships or scouts. I had men like Burt Moore, a grocery executive, who showed me how to read people, not just spreadsheets. Then there was Frank Mergle, a Romanian immigrant who worked at Tops Market and took a shine to me. Passionate, blunt, kind, and fiercely loyal, he often lectured high school kids on how lucky they were to be born here. On breaks, while teens unwrapped their Snickers, he'd lecture them on how lucky they were to be born here, giving them a crash course on gratitude.

What those kids didn't know was that Frank had risked his own life to escape Communism. Not only that—he shared with me once the story of how he smuggled fourteen other people out with him over the years. He never made a big deal out of what he'd done. But I knew. And I never forgot.

Early on, these two men taught me the same lesson: you can't lead a team if you're not on the team. Show up early. Do the grunt work. Lift others. Those lessons built every business I ever ran—and every friendship I've ever kept."

THURL:

"Being a part of a team was incredibly important to me. I felt on top of the world under a famous coach at NC State. But when he left the team, my mates and I felt bereft, ready to quit. I certainly didn't have a vision on my own. Enter Jim Valvano: a fast-talking Italian coach we'd never heard of. We sat there, arms crossed, faces blank, furious. He looked around and said, 'I know you don't want to be here. But I'm your new coach. Call me Coach V, and I'm going to win a national championship.'

We blinked. Excuse me?

'Give me 15 minutes,' he said. 'If you still want to quit, leave.' Fifteen minutes later, we were still listening. His vision, his voice, and his conviction had us hooked. Coach V didn't just talk championships; he made us *feel* them. On his desk? Gold scissors. Twice a month, he'd wheel out a ladder and make us rehearse cutting down the net like we'd won the championship, hoisting him over our heads and screaming like madmen. We laughed and felt ridiculous—until the night we actually did win it all, just three seasons later against Houston's NBA-bound giants. And from his vest pocket came those same golden scissors. Of course, we hoisted him over our heads. Of course, we screamed and clapped like madmen.

Coach V taught us to feel a dream before it comes true—to rehearse victory until it feels inevitable. That's not arrogance. That's belief. It shaped how I lead, how I parent, and how I approach every kid I mentor today. If you can't see it, you can't step into it. Practice victory."

JOHN:

"I never cut down a net, but I know the incredible power of *belief.* Growing up as 'just a laborer's kid,' plenty of people assumed I'd never build much, but I was out to prove them wrong. I didn't just work hard—I pictured the companies I wanted to build, the people I wanted to lift, and especially, because I loved kids, the causes I wanted to fund.

More often than not, those visions became reality because I refused to see any other outcome. It's not magic—it's grit paired with a picture of what's possible. When I bounced off a brick wall, it was the vision of what I was building that kept me going until it manifested."

THURL:

"Having someone believe in you is huge. Learning how to visualize and go after what you want in life is equally vital. But when others look at you solely on the color of your skin or where you came from, it can feel debilitating. It can shatter your spirit.

When I fell in love with Sindi—a ranch girl from Richfield, Utah—it wasn't just two worlds colliding. It was two cultures, two faiths, two races, and a tidal wave of family disapproval. The first time I went to meet her parents, they wouldn't even let me in the door.

Then came the night that changed everything.

Sindi went home for Family Home Evening—FHE, as they call it. But instead of games and lessons, it turned into an intervention. Her entire family was there, and ultimatums were on the table.

"It's him or us."

Sindi didn't flinch. She stood up and said, "I choose him."

I still get emotional thinking about that moment. That kind of love... that kind of bravery. She chose me over her entire family.

And I asked myself—*am I worthy of that?* What did she see in me that makes her willing to fight for this? I didn't feel worthy of her and couldn't stand the thought of estranging herself from her family. I even tried to break it off. But Sindi held the line and loved me fiercely until I gave in.

We married, enduring years of her family's silence, and built a life together—thirty-one years, three amazing kids, and, eventually, reconciliation. Sindi's parents apologized, welcomed me, and even thanked us for showing them what true love looks like."

JOHN:

"My first marriage was full of judgment. My in-laws saw me as a "do-nuthin'" who'd never amount to anything—certainly not provide for their daughter. Decades later, I'd built a thriving business, and they still didn't seem to respect me very much. Fortunately, I cared more about what Red and my mother thought of me, and they were proud of the man I'd become.

I told my kids two things: marry for love, no matter the background, and remember that some people teach you what to be—and some teach you what not to be."

Over the years, Thurl and I have worked side by side—on youth programs, concerts, foundations, and, yes, pickleball courts. (Fun fact: he's still mad that I introduced him to pickleball because now he's hooked.)

We've also shared some unforgettable laughs. Like the time we were hosting Utah's biggest country music event, Hot Country Nights. Thurl was towering over a sea of five-foot-four cowboys, and out of nowhere, he belted out to me, 'Play That Funky Music, White Boy!' I almost fell off the stage laughing.

But we've shared tears, too. On my 80th birthday (technically my 20th—as a leap year baby), Thurl headlined the night. Another friend opened, and Thurl closed, dedicating songs to our friendship. Standing there, choked up and hearing his voice and his words, I felt the full elation of something extraordinary:

At the end of the day, it's not your bank account, your skin color, or your trophies that matter. It's who you love. Who you show up for. Who you hold up when the world gets heavy.

What matters is what our parents, mentors, and lives have taught us:

- Listen to mentors who care and be accountable for your own results.
- Lead by lifting others. It's miraculous.
- Believe in the vision before it's real. Act like it's already happened.
- See the world through *love*, not fear. And embody that love wherever you go, whoever you get to influence, and make a difference. Even in a mad, chaotic world, it's possible. In fact, it's more important than ever.

The world needs more people like you and me to build bridges. Coretta Scott King said, 'The only way to build a bridge across division is through love strong enough to carry weight.' I learned how to build bridges in Jaycees, and it's continued ever since.

Thurl and I have created that bond specifically with our friendship, and there are times we have carried each other over those bridges. Believe us, the world needs many more 'beyond black and white' moments—where differences don't divide but create humor and harmony, and where belief makes the impossible feel inevitable.

Find your Thurl. Or find your John. Believe in something bigger than your past, and bigger than yourself. Then get to work building it.

As James Baldwin stated so powerfully: 'Not everything that is faced can be changed, but nothing can be changed until it is faced.'

Let's face it... together."

For more in-depth exploration of my friendship with Thurl, check out supplementary materials on our website: JohnAGullo.com.

CHAPTER 16:

My Adventure to Pickleball... Paddles, Passion, and Purpose

"Somewhere between an ambulance demanding cash and the hospital jimmy rigging a 20-foot oxygen hose from another patient, I realized: every day above ground is a gift—and service is the best way to say 'thank you'."
– John Gullo

It all started on October 31, 2008, while my wife Karen and I were in Puerto Rico for a Burger King meeting. On the very first day, adventure was calling, as usual. It didn't matter that I was 310 pounds. I hadn't let my increasing weight get in the way of any activities I ever wanted to do, so I set out to enjoy the beauty of the sea.

I was out snorkeling in the gorgeous turquoise waters 60 yards from shore—when suddenly I couldn't breathe. *What the hell?*

Terror and helplessness engulfed me. My heart started racing yet fluttering wildly, and my body felt like a lead weight in the water as exhaustion overtook me, and I still couldn't breathe. *I'm going to die.*

Fortunately, I was spotted flailing in the water. Karen assisted me as I kicked toward land. A water ambulance was called. To my dismay, there was no oxygen on board. Their advice? "Breathe deep, and we'll go fast."

Lucky for me, I used to scuba dive and always carried a waterproof pouch with cash around my neck because when we hit the dock, the emergency workers wouldn't let me off the boat until I gave them cash! Then the land ambulance refused treatment until I paid them in cash, too. At this point, I was desperate, feeling like a huge whale that had been spit up on dry land. It didn't matter that I was in cardiac arrest and was gasping for air; everyone was demanding money. It didn't stop there.

They provided me with the necessary oxygen, but when we finally reached a private hospital, the doctor approached me and said, "I work here, but I'm not affiliated. You have to pay me directly—in cash." *Enough already,* was all I could think.

Lying on the gurney, I was still covered in sand, so I asked for a shower. The orderly dropped me off and left me in the shower—no soap, no towel, no shampoo—where my wife eventually found me. Karen had to dry me off with the T-shirt I'd been wearing.

Back in the ER, the oxygen wasn't working. They rigged a 20-foot hose from the neighboring bed's tank. I called my friend, Dr. Charlie Lawton, in Utah, and handed the phone to the ER doc. "Did you run the enzyme test?" he asked. The doc said no. "Then how the hell do you know he's having a heart attack?"

My friend got back on the line. "Get the hell out of there. Fly to Utah now." Lucky for me, Karen was there to help me get out.

We left immediately.

From Salt Lake International Airport, I went straight to McKay-Dee Hospital. Three of my arteries were 30%, 60%, and 90% blocked. Just five hours later, I was having quintuple bypass surgery.

Leonard Cohen, a singer-songwriter who had a near-fatal heart incident, once said: “There is a crack in everything. That’s how the light gets in. The heart reminds you that nothing lasts forever—not fear, not pain, not even life. But if you’re lucky, you come out of it more aware.”

Well, my recovery started in St. George, Utah. They had me doing cardiac rehab on a treadmill—but it was painfully boring. Something needed to change, and my weight was no longer sustainable. Still, this treadmill thing was going to kill me off! My ADD couldn’t handle it, and I knew in my heart that in no time, I would be back to my previous behaviors and habits. And I knew I wouldn’t survive another heart attack.

That’s when I saw a sign in the gym that read, “Pickleball.”

Pickleball? I’ve never even heard of it.

Karen and I checked it out. I discovered the game was part tennis, part ping pong. It was played with a wiffle ball on a court a quarter of the size of a tennis court. Like me, few people had heard of it. Despite being 310 pounds, I started playing. In the meantime, I bent, stretched, and turned my head left and right. It wasn’t long before I thought, *This is a blast!*—and it was working. I started shedding weight.

Being competitive, I wanted to be good. Someone told me, “You can’t be good at this game overnight.”

My response? “Just wait till I come back in the fall!”

My doctor and friend, Brett Muse, said, “John worked hard. He basically turned himself around and did an amazing job. For somebody who was really struggling along with diabetes and heart disease… to a better lifestyle, better management of diets, and a lot more exercise too. They’re really important and they’re hard to do. There’s no question. I deal with it every day. They’re not easy, but if anybody can do it, it’s John Gullo. He puts his mind to something, and it’s going to happen.” And now I had both my health and pickleball to think of.

I had a lot of time to consider my life. It was a miracle I was still breathing. I remembered what it was like to grow up in the Italian sector of Buffalo, New York. Back then, a lot of Sicilian-American kids looked up to mafia figures. I was one of them. But in that twist of fate, I joined the Jaycees, where I learned that "service to humanity is the best work of life." That philosophy had been my compass ever since, I realized, and it didn't have to stop now!

Even while building my Burger King franchise business, I'd always kept one eye on my community. While I loved supporting kids, schools, firefighters, and folks with disabilities through the American Dream Foundation, I had no idea how pickleball would quickly become one of my greatest avenues for service.

Just six months later, in May 2009, I met with Ogden Mayor Matt Godfrey and offered to pay for the first eight public pickleball courts in Northern Utah. Usually, red tape would've meant it would take over a year just to approve my donation, but Matt leased me the land at Mount Ogden Park. One more time, I told Karen, "Let's do this!" By July, the Gullo Pickleball Grotto was complete.

To introduce the sport, I placed an ad in the paper and invited people out. Karen and Phil Wisner responded—they already knew the game and offered to help. I brought in a United States of America Pickleball Association (USAPA) ambassador and top player, Tim Finger, to give us a demo. About 150 people showed up. Why? Because I fed them. (Burger King perks!)

Once the pros were done, we opened the courts and let people try the game. Some of them stayed out under the lights until 10:30 that night! I could feel it in my bones; it was the start of something big.

We formed the Ogden Pickleball Club as a nonprofit. I also converted one of my warehouses into an indoor court for winter play—$100 per person, run on the honor system. No staff. It worked like a charm. We were packed!

From there, we expanded courts into over ten Utah cities—now over 400 public courts in Northern Utah alone—and helped build them in places like Alpine, Wyoming. I even taught people how to play in Madrid, Spain. We provided equipment like balls and custom paddles to every junior high and high school in the Ogden School District, as well as to organizations like the YMCA, Youth Impact, and the Boys and Girls Club. We even helped get pickleball lines painted in local LDS church gyms so people could play indoors during winter. The ripple of health, fitness, connection, relationships, and competition continued. But it went deeper than that.

We hosted sessions for kids with disabilities. That might have been my favorite thing. Watching them play and smile—and seeing local players volunteer and walk away changed—it reminded me why I love this sport, and what service does to the human soul.

Beginning around 2011, I helped develop Brigham City, Utah's first courts, which would eventually become the home of our Tournament of Champions (TOC). We added four more courts with help from Weber County RAMP Tax, along with my foundation, and the Ogden Pickleball Association.

Then I had the idea: What if we held a *pro* tournament?

We offered $18,000 in prize money and invited 36 top players. They loved it. After Dennis Forbes, my dear friend and main contributor to our pickleball association, passed away, we renamed the tournament the Dennis Forbes Memorial. By 2013, 90 top players competed. The prize pool was $38,000.

That's when Pro Pickleball was born.

I launched the Professional Pickleball Federation (PPF), bringing together over 300 professionals. I remembered all the lessons my beloved mentor, Mal Kennedy, had shared with me about his time in the NFL. I learned from his failures and his triumphs.

So, we held tournaments in Palm Springs, Florida, Bend, Oregon, and of course, Brigham City. It was a little early—sponsorship dollars weren't there yet, and I hired the wrong guy to run it. Still, it lit the match.

I personally funded a paddle company, Pickleball Now. We were the first to get into Dick's Sporting Goods. Escalade Sports acquired us and shortly after, Onix, who kept the Onix name. As part of the deal, they sponsored The Tournament of Champions (TOC) for two years—$20,000 per year. That was a first in the sport.

In 2014, we changed divisions: Masters became Pro. Legends became Senior Pro.

I sold TOC to Brigham City—making it the first pickleball tournament ever sold for money. The city added six more courts and one more championship court. At its height, TOC hosted 200 pros and over 600 amateurs with a $100,000 prize pool! I was delighted to write the checks.[8] We even hosted a scholarship tournament for juniors, where I contributed $25,000 to help the next generation. Unfortunately, after a couple of decades together, Karen and I, who had been growing distant, parted ways for good due to irreconcilable differences. Pickleball, however, continued growing even stronger.

In 2019, I told a television producer and reporter that Pickleball was destined to be the fastest-growing sport in the nation. He was charmed by my passion, but even then, he shook his head. I explained, "You don't see that competitive 'I gotta beat you' kind of thing... even in doubles, you'll see partners changing from tournament to tournament. It's social; even at the highest level, it's social. The respect factor is there."

"How long do you foresee that staying that way with pickleball?" the producer asked, "because we're talking about more tennis players coming in, and tennis is known as more of an isolated sport. How long do you see that being the norm in pickleball?"

"At this level," I shared, "the pro level, the players are changing about every eighteen months. So, my gut feel—if I had to gamble—I'd say that in about six years, you'll see these events closed, you'll see them—"

"Closed?" he said, surprised, cutting me off.

"In other words, you won't get to see them for free; you're going to have to pay to be there. It started at Nationals last year..."

"You're saying in six years you think?"

"Six years I think it's going to be in its fruition."

And I was right.

Pickleball has literally exploded over the past few years—not just as a backyard pastime, but as a global sport and industry! Pickleheads

---

8 Austin Curtright, "Pro pickleball tour comes to Utah for annual Tournament of Champions," *The Salt Lake Tribune*, August 15, 2023, https://www.sltrib.com/sports/2023/08/15/pro-pickleball-tour-comes-utah/.

(an online forum for pickleball enthusiasts) estimated in 2024 that there were 19.8 million active players—up a staggering 45.8% from 2023 and 311% growth since 2021. And in terms of that growth, it didn't hurt that there are now somewhere between 68,000 and 70,000 pickleball courts in the U.S., with a 55% increase in new dedicated facilities in one year (2024) alone, and it has been the fastest-growing sport in all of America in the last five years.[9]

Through it all, I've stuck to one mantra: "Play hard, work hard, and do something for your community."

In 2024, I was inducted into the Pickleball Hall of Fame. The ceremony was held in Mesa, Arizona, and let me tell you—what an honor. Standing there with so many of the people who've built this sport from the ground up, I was deeply humbled and moved. Some of the greatest people and players of all time reside in that Hall of Fame, and I didn't take their decades of hard work for granted. None of us did this alone.

As I looked out over the room of Pickleball supporters and friends, at my whole family, including my son Johnny, my grandkids, and great grandkids, I was overcome. I knew two things: First, the understanding that service changes people's lives. It sculpts them into better, more compassionate, more heart-centered people. Second, that pickleball, my own personal miracle, was becoming a miracle in hearts and minds and courts around the world.

For example, I remember when, seven years ago, a young 11-year-old phenom, a pickleball prodigy, won gold in my Tournament of Champions. What an honor to place the ring on her finger. I realized then, she was the next best thing since 7-Up. She is now the number one female pickleball player in the U.S. Anna Leigh Waters recently signed a contract with Nike.[10]

---

9 Brandon Mackie, "Pickleball statistics – the numbers behind America's fastest-growing sport," Pickleheads, February 19, 2025, https://www.pickleheads.com/guides/pickleball-statistics.

10 Jessica Golden, "Nike signs phenom Anna Leigh Waters in its first pickleball deal," *CNBC Sport*, January 13, 2026, https://www.cnbc.com/2026/01/13/nike-anna-leigh-waters-pickleball-deal.html.

I never expected one little paddle and plastic ball to transform my life and quite literally, my heart. But it did. And aside from my grandchildren and great-grandchildren, this has been one of the most joyful surprises of all.

"John is completely unconstrained, right? He is not an out-of-the-box thinker, he doesn't know where the box is. John is very good at problem-solving. Some of the things that he was wanting to do in the venues had never been allowed before. So, we were trying to figure out how to make it all work, and how to create this vision in a way that was palatable to neighbors: government officials, the health department, the parks department, insurance, everybody. We had to figure out how to put all these pieces together in a way that had never been accomplished before... And then he did it."

– Matt Godfrey, former Mayor of Ogden City[11]

11 Printed with recorded permission by Matt Godfrey.

CHAPTER 17:

Mexico, My New Home... (And New Life)

"I slept and dreamt that life was joy. I awoke and saw that life was service. I acted, and behold, service was joy."
– Rabindranath Tagore

Almost ten years ago, I went to a charity auction for Youth Impact. One of the prizes was a week's stay at a resort in Baja, Mexico. I raised my hand, placed my bid, and won. At the time I thought, *Well, this will be a nice little winter escape.* Having grown up in New York and then spent decades in Utah, I was used to winters being something you endured, not enjoyed. I had no clue that one little trip would end up changing the entire rhythm of my life.

The resort was Pueblo Sunset Beach, and it was something else. Sprawling villas, executive suites, even luxury four-bedroom homes, plus seven restaurants, were scattered across the property. It was sunshine, turquoise water, and the kind of warmth that seeps into your bones. I was hooked. For the next six years straight, I went back every January, February, and half of March. I thought, *Life doesn't get any better than this.*

But then came pickleball.

One year, my friend Scott Moore—who happens to be a professional pickleball player—told me about a little town up the coast called Los Barriles. "They've even got a pickleball facility for sale," he said. We drove up to take a look. I didn't buy the facility, but I fell in love with the town.

Los Barriles was small—only about 7,000 people—and 60 percent of them were expat Canadians and Americans. There was only one paved road running right along the Sea of Cortez, and that was enough. The place reminded me of Star Valley in Wyoming, where I spent summers cooling off in the mountain air. It hit me then: I'm just not a big-city guy. And the good news? I didn't have to be.

So, I bought a house.

It was a beautiful place with an adjacent lot. Like most houses there, it was walled and gated. At first, I thought, *Well, that makes sense. Must be a security thing.* But I soon learned how wrong I was.

One evening, a girlfriend of mine and I were sitting by the pool. The ocean shimmered turquoise in the distance, the sky streaked orange and purple. Everything was still and peaceful—until we heard a shuffle, then a snort, then the sound of hooves. Out of the shadows came a whole herd of cows, lumbering past as if they owned the neighborhood. One big steer even stopped, looked right at me, and chewed slowly, as if to say, *"Nice roses you've got there, amigo. Shame if something happened to them."*

I burst out laughing. That's when it clicked. The walls and gates weren't for security. They were to keep the livestock from turning our gardens into an all-you-can-eat buffet.

Only in Mexico.

Of course, moving into a new home in another country wasn't without challenges. The first three months were rough. The inspection had missed a few things—well, more than a few—and the seller had played games. Then came my introduction to the true meaning of the word *mañana*.

In the States, mañana means "tomorrow." In Mexico, it means "not today." Sometimes it meant tomorrow, sometimes three days later, sometimes next week if the fishing was good. I'd call for service on a Monday, and by Thursday, a crew would show up as cheerful as could be, acting as if we had agreed to that exact time.

At first, it drove me crazy. But here's the thing: when they finally did arrive, their work was excellent. They didn't rush. They took pride in doing it right. That's when I learned my first big Mexican lesson—find the right people, treat them well, and they'll take care of you. And laugh about mañana instead of cursing it.

By my second year, I was settled. My business mind, of course, started looking around. I thought about buying lots to flip for profit. In the process, I met a realtor who mentioned the *bomberos*—the volunteer fire department—were planning to build a fire hall south of town. The catch? They didn't have a fire engine.

That struck a chord. My father had been a firefighter, and I'd worked with departments back in Ogden. The plan was to buy a used truck in California and drive it down. I stepped in and said, "Let me buy it." I also shared some of the programs we used in Utah schools—boots and bunkers education, fire prevention, and safety outreach for kids. It felt like a natural continuation of something that had always been in my blood.

The town's medical clinic impressed me as well. It was clean, efficient, and staffed with good people—but their ambulance was on its last legs, and the nearest hospital was ninety minutes away in Los Cabos. When I learned someone had offered to match funds to buy a new ambulance if another donor stepped up, I jumped at the chance.

When the purchase was finished, I looked the director of the East Cape Clinic in the eye and said, "Now, the three most important things you need to remember are: First, Casa Diamante—that's my house name, since we don't use street addresses here. Second, Gullo. And third, 'Large Contributor.' If you ever get a call that mentions my house or my name, your job is to get that ambulance up there, pronto."

I said it with a grin, but I wasn't entirely joking. At my age, fast access to an ambulance wasn't just convenient—it could be life-saving. Was it charitable? Absolutely. Was it self-serving? Maybe a little. But after what I'd seen in Puerto Rico, I knew the value of paying it forward when it came to emergency care!

My heart has always gone out to kids, so when I discovered how education worked in Mexico, it floored me. If children want to attend 12th grade, it costs the family $500. College is $1,000 a year. For families already struggling to put food on the table, that might as well be a million. The East Cape Guild was raising funds to send kids to school. I started donating, then got more involved. By 2023, this little community raised enough to send 240 kids to school. For a town of about 7,000 people, that was nothing short of miraculous.

I loved the expat community in Los Barriles. These were big-hearted people who gave back generously. But it was the locals who impressed me most. They reminded me of my New York neighborhood growing up: families sticking together, working hard, leaning on faith. Poverty didn't rob them of dignity. When you gave a gratuity, they accepted it with gratitude, never expectation. Entitlement wasn't in their vocabulary.

That's why, when I heard about Leaders2Give, I was drawn in. It was a U.S. nonprofit, founded by expats, raising money for different projects in Baja. One initiative in particular stopped me cold.

In the town of El Cardinal, north of Los Barriles, land had been donated to build a children's home—for kids whose parents or siblings were being treated for life-threatening illnesses and forced to be away from home. In Mexico, the three big killers are heart disease, diabetes, and cancer. Without a welfare system, families already drowning in poverty had nowhere to turn. Kids were left adrift.

I knew what desperation felt like. I knew what it was to be poor, and have at least one parent out of the picture. This project hit me deeply.

I ended up donating a significant amount to get the construction going and pledged to cover part of the operating budget for the first three years. More importantly, I promised to stay involved personally. I wanted to see the kids thrive, not just hear about it in reports.

And yes, I even thought, *Maybe I'll build them a pickleball court someday.*

By 2023, I'd become a permanent resident of Mexico. My plan was to live there for six to seven months a year. I didn't want to just soak up the sunshine; I wanted to keep spotting opportunities to make a difference.

Leaders2Give put out an official statement about my contributions as "a testament to John's legacy of philanthropy and humanitarianism [and] his belief that every child deserves love, care, and a safe place to grow—no matter their circumstances."

As for me, I dreamed a better dream for kids, and being involved was proof once again that service can be joy. I could care less about my name being on a project or a building, but I have always believed that with committed hearts, certain legacies will last far beyond our lifetimes.

"He's got the biggest heart of anyone I've ever met. He's so generous, and he cares so much about people; it's where he lives and his passions. It's really too bad that more people don't know that; they know he's done a lot of good things. And he's put money in places that really needed it and supported a lot of neat things. But I think they don't really realize what a big-hearted kind of teddy bear he is. He's very brash on the outside, but he has a huge heart, and it's always in the right place. And... when John says, 'we're doing it?' We're doing it."

– Natalie Summers, Administrator Extraordinaire[12]

12 Printed with permission by Natalie Summers, December 2025.

EPILOGUE:

And Now the End Is Near… Or Maybe Not!

"In Mexico, time slows down so your heart can catch up."
— Anonymous

One January morning in 2024, my phone rang. A friend's voice came on the line, half laughing, half warning.

"John, you're not going to believe this. I just read a story about a stolen painting discovered in a house during an estate sale in St. George… and guess who owned the house?"

I joked, "Let me guess—someone with a last name that rhymes with *trouble*?"

When I heard what he shared next, my eyes popped open wider than a kid staring at the dessert table after Sunday dinner.

The late estate owner? My only and oldest brother Jim—Jim Gullo.

I went online, and the news was everywhere: an 18th-century oil painting called *The Schoolmistress,* painted by English artist John Opie around 1784, had been stolen from a home in Newark, New Jersey, on July 25, 1969. Three men tied to the mafia carried it off, allegedly under the direction of Anthony Imperiale, a New Jersey state senator with strong mob ties. At the time, the painting had been purchased during the Depression by Dr. Earl Leroy Wood for $7,500—a fortune in those days. After a failed first burglary attempt on a coin collection, the thieves came back and succeeded, spiriting the 40-by-50-inch canvas into the shadows of organized crime.

And then it vanished. For decades, it was passed around like contraband poker chips, shuffled from one set of mob-connected hands to another.[13]

Fast forward to 1989. Jim bought a house in Hallandale Beach, Florida, from Joseph Covello Sr., a convicted mobster tied to the Gambino crime family. Included in the sale, though they think Jim probably never realized it, was *The Schoolmistress*. He later moved it to his home in St. George, Utah, where it hung quietly on his wall for years.

After Jim's death in 2020, an accounting firm appraising his estate spotted the painting and raised an eyebrow. The FBI got involved. After a two-year investigation, they confirmed the painting's identity and traced it back to the Wood family.

In January 2024, in a courtroom in Utah, a judge ruled the painting belonged to the heirs of Dr. Wood. Days later, FBI Special Agent Gary France stood in Newark, New Jersey, and handed the painting to Dr. Francis Wood, the 96-year-old son of the original owner. The FBI called it one of the most unique and intriguing cases they'd ever handled. The painting was in remarkable shape, with only minor paint loss, despite being in homes where its true value was never recognized. Its return was celebrated as a major moment in the Wood family's history.[14]

What I wouldn't have given to be there!

No charges were filed—everyone involved in the theft had long since died.

When I read the story, I shook my head and thought: *Of course.*

---

13 Andy Rose, "Precious painting stolen by mobsters returned to rightful owner after more than 50 years, the FBI says," CNN, January 29, 2024, https://www.cnn.com/2024/01/29/us/the-schoolmistress-stolen-painting-returned.

14 Ibid.

When you get older, you ponder things more deeply, I think, and I simply had to recognize that Jim and I had lived parallel lives—often intertwined, but pulling in opposite directions from the time we were young. While Jim gravitated toward mobsters and darkness, I'm so grateful I'd discovered so early on that I didn't have to follow him there. I detested the way he often treated others, and often bragged to me that he'd still been up to his shenanigans until he passed—like buying a Mercedes and paying cash for it under the table to avoid taxes.

I sighed then, in understanding. I felt like Jim was always ruled by the dollar. Though we opened a store in Washington County, we didn't own the ground but owned the building. After 20 years, I recommended we let go of the lease.

I took good care of him, but all I felt was relief when I didn't have to be my brother's landlord anymore.

After Jim's death, that stolen painting became a kind of symbol for me. Jim couldn't even recognize the most "priceless" thing in his home, which I would argue was not the painting; it was his family. He operated on shortcuts and shadows, and he didn't understand how to profit from the fruits of his labor. Me? I got lucky. If it hadn't been for Red and the Jaycees, *I* might have been that man. Red taught me integrity. The Jaycees taught me service. Together, they rerouted the whole trajectory of my life.

It's been almost four years since I began writing this memoir. Sifting through my own memories and listening to the voices of those who shaped me has brought more self-awareness than I expected. Funny thing—looking back has been the best way to chart my way forward.

I'll admit, both of my marriages ending have been the greatest tragedies of my personal life. But from the first came my two sons, who remain my greatest joy. Even when we don't agree (and believe me, that's not rare), I am deeply proud of the men they've become. I realized it during that 20th Leap Year birthday party—celebrated at age 80 when Johnny was recorded saying, "Dad's not only unique, forthcoming, and honest, he speaks his mind. What my grandfather instilled in him, he instilled in me: give back. We're here for a short time, and we're grateful for what we have. And we enjoy giving back."

Hearing my son define *his* life with that answer—that was one of the proudest moments of mine. Martin Luther King Jr. once said, "Life's most persistent and urgent question is: What are you doing for others?" Johnny knows what he is doing in the world. He keeps giving to others, but it surprised me when Johnny compared me to Larry H. Miller: jeans, plain shirt, no showboating—but always giving. That one warmed me straight through. Larry was a good man.

When I was inducted into the Pickleball Hall of Fame, turnabout was fair play. I made sure to give Johnny credit. Truth is, I was only able to accomplish what I did in ADF and Pickleball because of *him*. We don't always see eye-to-eye, but beneath everything is a deep, mutual respect that I will cherish forever.

* * *

Now, let's talk about dating at 80. Being single was no different than being single at 20—except it sucked a lot more. Some women worried I was looking for a nurse. I'd grin and say, "You think you can keep up with me?" Humor has always been my secret weapon.

The truth was, I had a 20-year-old mind in an 80-year-old body. I won't say which was holding up better. But I could still land a one-liner faster than most people can finish a sentence. Still, after two marriages, I almost gave up. I'd never been a player. I wanted one woman for life... but that didn't seem likely anymore.

And then, just after my 20th Leap Year birthday, life surprised me again. Literally. I stopped in Surprise, Arizona, on my way back from Mexico. Friends of mine, Stryker and Robin Dunda, wanted me to meet someone. I groaned, "No way. I'm done."

Spoiler alert: I wasn't.

That's when I met René Villeneuve Jenkins.

She was everything I wasn't expecting—sharp, funny, with a firecracker wit. A progressive, through and through, while I am a fiscal-conservative-die-hard-Trump fan. But the banter? Downright electric. She laughed at my sarcasm, parried my jokes, and threw her own right back. We discovered that despite politics, we were far more alike than different.

Quickly, she recognized that when I made errors, they were errors of the mind, but not the heart. Despite my being rough around the edges, she noticed people often genuinely respected me and respected my honesty. I share *everything*, as my kids know better than anyone else.

One day, René kissed me and said, "You really make me feel like a woman." If that didn't stroke the ego, I don't know what else could.

I wasn't looking for somebody, and she wasn't looking for somebody. God, however, was looking out for both of us. Our hearts lined up. Our laughter lined up. Our affection, too, and these last two years? Bliss.

Life really can begin at 80.

Marta, a good friend who first tried to help me with my memoir, once called me a "lane-changer." She was right. My mind has always darted from one topic and one challenge to the next. But these days, the challenge isn't fixing everything myself—it's finding fulfillment without carrying all the weight.

Here's what I've learned: I give. I teach. I mentor. I help others build their projects without needing to be the one in charge. Sometimes I step in when I have to, and even that keeps me sharp and far from bored. I love. I laugh. I play pickleball almost every day. René and I pair up for doubles, and my dink shot—soft, controlled, sneaky—still surprises the best of them. That's been my life, really: surprising people who underestimate me.

I've hired a trainer so I can keep up with René and the grandkids–plus seven great-grandchildren now! They're my fuel, my joy, my living legacy. What more could a man ask for?

Like Sinatra said, "I did it my way." But let's be honest. For me, it's more like: "I *dinked* it my way." (If you don't know what that means, it's a pickleball term.)

And just to prove pickleball still has tricks up its sleeve, I recently was placed in a position where I'm heavily involved in pickleball associations, tournaments, and events again. Not kidding. But that's another story.

A better one is how I recently proposed to René.

Spoiler alert: She said yes.

We went to celebrate at a rodeo. At one point, I glanced at my phone, and a rodeo clown caught me… he thought I was scrolling.

"Dude!" he bellowed over the loudspeaker. "Watch the rodeo, not your phone! Especially when the show is hot, and you've got a pretty lady beside you!"

I stood up, grinning, and held up my phone. "I agree! I was just answering friends congratulating us on our engagement!"

Suddenly, he put us up on the Jumbotron, announcing our engagement. The crowd erupted, with 7,000 strangers cheering like they'd been invited to the wedding. René leaned in, wide-eyed. "Did you plan this? Paid him off?"

I laughed. "Nope. These things just happen. Remember what my friend Karen Wisner said about my golden horseshoe? And where it resides?"

And imagining just that, René just laughed and laughed. "Oh, John. You wouldn't be able to sit down!"

At that moment, despite my chuckles, chills raced down my spine. I spent too much of my life chasing my next big win. But standing there, beside René, I finally understood the full miracle about the "golden horseshoe." It wasn't about luck or spectacle. It was about learning to treasure what's right in front of you. René was my golden gift—loving me as I was, sharp edges and all. She was the treasure I might have missed if I hadn't learned to see… and listen.

That's what love, service, and legacy come down to: not letting the priceless moments pass unnoticed.

As of February 2026, René and I tied the knot. We finalized our loving commitment to one another. It wasn't performed in front of 7,000 people, but in our dear friend's home, with a small circle of loved ones around us. That was just the beginning of a beautiful life together. Today, René and I split time between Los Barriles, Star

Valley, and the occasional European adventure… and I'll never stop serving a worthy cause.

Albert Schweitzer once said, "The only ones who will be really happy are those who have sought and found how to serve." I'll add: too many people today are motivated by the dollar, not the dream. The richest among us are the ones who learn to see the gold already at their feet.

So, here's my final invitation:

Find what lights you up.

Find what makes you laugh.

Find what keeps you grounded in gratitude.

Then serve the hell out of it.

Because if I've learned anything, it's this: service is joy. And love is the treasure we carry home.

Acknowledgements

"If I have seen further, it is by standing on the shoulders of giants."
— Sir Isaac Newton

After I'd checked off a good number of life boxes—building businesses, dodging disasters, doing some good in the world—a surprising number of people began telling me I should write my life story. Either they saw value in it… or they just wanted proof that half of it actually happened.

One evening, while attending a concert headlined by my very talented friend Terah Taylor, I happened to be seated next to a publisher from Sacramento. Martha Zarrella listened to a clip of me giving a speech to the IRS (yes, the IRS, of all places), and decided it sounded like the beginning of something worth publishing. We began to work together, but then along came the 2020 pandemic, and like everything else in the world, our plans were thrown into chaos.

Now, I could have shelved the whole book project, blamed the pandemic, and walked away. But by then, too many interviews had been conducted and too many stories told to let them vanish into thin air. So, I went in search of someone brave enough and curious enough to tackle this story with me.

That's when I reconnected with Bridget Cook-Burch, a NYT bestselling author and publisher, who guides people through writing stories that matter. We'd met over a decade earlier during some nonprofit mischief (the good kind) at a derby, and teaming up on this book turned out to be a full-circle moment. She asked the hard questions, helped me wrangle the timeline, and kept this train on the tracks. I will never be able to repay her for her efforts in completing this book.

The person I need to thank most of all is my son Johnny, who held down the fort and kept my other activities on target. In reality, he has become my business manager. He's played such an integral role in my business career and my charitable activity throughout much of what I have accomplished, and his follow-through on projects I created has made them successful.

I also want to thank Natalie Summers, my ever-patient assistant, who helped me navigate just about everything—from calendars to common sense. She tempered my bold, direct personality, translated my big ideas into action, and was the glue, the gears, and the grace behind much of what we built at the American Dream Foundation.

- Scott Conley, past Lieutenant, Ogden Police Department, who supplemented and guided me through creating all the inner-city projects for youth.
- Former Mayor Matthew Godfrey, whose support and approval of my ideas made Hot Rock'n 4th, Hot Country Nights, and pickleball in Ogden possible.
- Robert Bell, who became a great friend, even while he provided me with the printing materials for all my activities and his guidance and helped me get elected to the Ogden City School Board.
- Trent Christopherson, not only my broker but the man who got me on my first board membership with Enable Industries, which also gave me the foundation to develop my own nonprofit.
- Harlan Schmidt and Brett Dagley, the CPAs who wisely guided me through my business activities and taught me so much. Harlan said, "John, you make things black and white faster than anyone I've ever known," and he saw how it served the whole.

- Bob Brooks, who taught me the golden rule (different from Red's), "If you've got the gold, you make the rules," and he became an important financial partner and advisor, especially in cash management during construction.
- Neil Saban, my attorney, who made sure that what I did was within the law and ethical. This was important because I always believed that asking forgiveness was easier than asking for permission.
- Don Belnap, past President of the Ogden City School Board. Together, we got a vital bond passed for the Ogden City School District—one which had been defeated in the past. We became tight friends, and I'll celebrate knowing him for life.
- Charlie Lawton, my doctor, neighbor, and friend, who jumped in after my bypass surgery and helped me to become healthier. His objective criticism of things I said and did was inspiring, even though we didn't always agree!
- Dennis Forbes, my partner in creating Professional Pickleball. Unfortunately, he passed before it became reality, but I know he would be proud of the legacy of today.
- Bringing Pickleball to northern Utah could not have ever happened without the following people jumping in: Phil and Karen Wisner, Carl and Dora Henniger, Neil Citty, Mike and Nadine McKay, Terry & Karla Corbridge, and Judy Morris.
- The creation of Professional Pickleball could not have happened without Jeff and Lynn Gardner, Bob and Jetty Lanius, Wayne and Nancy Muggli, Kristy Wolford, Kyle Klein, Harvey Dalton Lynn and Linda Laymon, Melissa McCurley, Byron and Marcia Freso, Bonnie Williams, Dave Weinbach, and Winnie Montgomery.
- Special thanks to the first professional pickleball players who saw my vision: Hilary Marold, Jennifer Lucore, Enrique Ruiz, Kyle Yates, Scott Moore, Alex Hamner, Tim Nelson, Wes Gabrielsen, Gigi LeMaster, Dave Weinbach, and so many more! All, I might add, are in the Pickleball Hall of Fame!

- I deeply acknowledge Bill Francis, my videographer and close friend, who helped put real-life videos of every function and charity I've ever supported, and who has witnessed miracles alongside me.
- Special thanks to Jennifer Cowin Jones (JJ), who produced the majority of all my nonprofit videos and helped me in the production of Hot Rock'n 4th.
- Special thanks to all the business and professional associates through the years who collaborated with me and mentored me, who later granted interviews and triggered vital memories of things past: Tom Mueller, former President of Wendy's Corporation; Carrie Fullerton, my loan officer at Bank of Utah; Rick Cowley, franchisee in the Burger King Corporation; Thurl Bailey, Utah Jazz player, Keynote, and Musician; Henry Marsh, Olympian and Keynote.
- Deep appreciation for the public relations genius of Doug Jardine, who manages all my PR for all of my various activities—pickleball, charities, music, and more.
- My Beta Readers, Tom Maris Dyer, Gigi LeMaster, Karen Wisner, and Janet Cheney, gave me honest and real feedback to make this book better, and perhaps to reach more ordinary souls who get to live extraordinary lives because of you.
- And finally, to everyone who played a part in the stories, miracles, messes, and memories found in these pages—thank you. You know who you are, and if you don't, just assume I'm talking about you and take the credit!!

About the Authors

"If I can't dazzle them with my brilliance,
I baffle them with my bullshit."
— unattributed, and adopted by John Gullo

John Gullo was born and raised in Buffalo, New York, and then Niagara Falls, where his street smarts turned to business savvy as he first worked his way up in Tops Market, a grocery chain, as a meatcutter, then department manager, then manager over several departments. Having a greater desire for his wife and family, he took a huge risk to enter the restaurant business. He made an impressive contribution over four and a half years at Burger King before he took the plunge to become a Burger King franchisee. No one, including John, knew just how big a Burger King empire he would build in his career, but he wasn't satisfied with only building restaurants. John loved to build people. Even as his staff were flipping Whoppers, John was flipping entire communities, launching dozens of nonprofit projects for kids, families, schools, firefighters with a massive patriotic flair in his nonprofit, The American Dream Foundation.

Even then, life didn't let John off easily. At 310 pounds, a snorkeling trip ended in congestive heart failure and five bypasses. Instead of taking up crossword puzzles, John took up pickleball. Always seeing opportunity to serve, even as he dropped a hundred pounds, he started building pickleball courts all over northern Utah, and purposely helped invent the professional side of the sport. To this day, he's been called a philanthropist, an entrepreneur, the father of pro pickleball, and "the Burger King with a heart." He calls himself something simpler: a guy who works hard, plays harder, and never turns down dessert, especially if it's chocolate cannoli.

You can reach John Gullo on his website, www.JohnAGullo.com and on Facebook at https://www.facebook.com/john.gullo.7

Clients call Bridget Cook-Burch "The Book Whisperer" — not just because she helps people write books, but because she helps them hear the deeper truth inside their own stories.

A New York Times and Wall Street Journal bestselling author, publisher, mentor, humanitarian, and speaker, Bridget is known for guiding powerful transformations through story. Her work has been featured on Oprah, Dateline, Netflix, Discovery+, A&E, Paramount+, CNN, GMA, NPR, and in People, among many others.

But her real work began the moment her own life cracked open. After a profound near-death experience, Bridget realized the story she had been living - and the one she had been telling herself - were not the same. That awakening set her on a path to uncover the extraordinary within the ordinary, and to help others do the same.

As CEO and Founder of Your Inspired Story and Inspired Legacy Publishing, Bridget creates spaces where people feel safe enough to tell the truth... and brave enough to transform it. Through immersive retreats, executive book mentoring and deeply experiential work, she guides writers, leaders, and visionaries into the stories that change everything.

Her greatest passion is helping you recognize the power of your own story—and step into the kind of leadership that ripples through families, communities, and the world.

Learn more at www.YourInspiredStory.com.

Reviews

"John Gullo is a unique person and friend. His book is very inspirational and it will provide motivation to many entrepreneurs, fathers, grandfathers, students, teachers and more. I recommend reading, digesting and comparing John's story to your own story. Then, reading it again. It's worth it."

—Tom Mueller

24-year Burger King Veteran, Former President and COO, Wendy's International, Inc.

"John Gullo's memoir is not only a fascinating story about a man who has overcome numerous obstacles and challenges in life, but who has also taken every opportunity to make this world a better place, and to make the people around him better people. This is a delightful read, filled with humor and honesty, life's disappointments and successes, mistakes made and wisdom gained. If everyone followed John's "Lessons to Live By," what an amazing world it would be! "Thank you" is not enough appreciation for all the contributions and lasting impacts that John has already made. So I'll just say it again. Thank you, John."

—Fran Myer

Author and 2018 Pickleball Hall of Fame Inductee

"I found it to be beautifully written and engaging throughout. The book is a fascinating insight into the formation of John's strong character, his willingness to take risks for the betterment of himself and others, and his genuinely warm heart. Now I know why it was so easy for my husband and me to become dear friends with John. He is a true visionary and pioneer—the driving force behind introducing professional pickleball, which has now exploded the sport astronomically. His story is inspiring, and the book is full of meaningful life lessons that resonate long after reading."
—Marsha Freso
USAP former Director of Referees and Ambassador

"John's story was very honest and inspiring. His ideas and creativity shone throughout his life, from saving money to buy Christmas presents for his family at a young age to the Rockin' 4th celebrations. The life lessons at the end of each chapter cause you to reflect on his experiences.
For me, it was an insight into the man my mother recently married."
—Leslie Hooks
Family Friend

"It is a fun, engaging read that was truly hard to put down. Even ten years after meeting him, I realized my knowledge of his life was just the tip of the iceberg. The more I read, the more the word WOW crept in. From horses to Snickers, and everything in between, as well as family man to philanthropist, his story is remarkable. In my mind and my heart, the title should actually be The Extraordinary Adventures of an Extraordinary Man. Thank you, John Gullo, for all you are and all you've done and all you have yet to do."
—Nora Chetterbock
Pickleball Enthusiast

"As a fellow entrepreneur and friend of John Gullo, I devoured this raw memoir. From Buffalo's rat-infested tenements and street-smart wise guy hustles to building real businesses and the American Dream Foundation, John holds nothing back—raw humor, brutal lessons, zero sugarcoating. That same fire once got him in trouble, but became rocket fuel for his empire and his drive to lift others. Thurl Bailey's foreword nails it: an ordinary man turned adversity into generosity and legacy. Street-to-boardroom wisdom every founder needs."

—Mark Stiegemeier

World Freestyle Skiing Champion, Business Founder, and Technology Inventor

---

"I have been close friends with John for about 15 years ... I thought I knew who John Gullo was! This book was a joy to read, and easily and eagerly read each chapter, looking forward to the life lessons John would share. I loved how each chapter of his life began with a powerful quote!

I knew that John was philanthropic and generous... I knew about his theory on making sure his community always benefitted while he created a legal win for himself. Oh and the government gets left out of the funds because John's brain thinks faster and smarter than almost anyone I know... his accomplishments are extraordinary and his generosity is unmatched by anyone!

I see this book as a great leadership book! John's life experiences are disclosed in a chronological way, and each chapter is an opportunity to learn more about this extraordinary man. I feel privileged to call John Gullo my friend!"

—Pat Nissan

MST Marriage and Family Therapist

*"What an outstanding journey!
Reading the adventures and lessons in the life of John Gullo has really inspired me. He is a master at thinking outside the box and implementing!
I thought I knew John. Boy, was I wrong! There are so many life lessons and experiences that can assist others along their own journey in this book. I think the book could be in the self-help section. I'm anxious to get a copy in the hands of a few of our kids who will definitely learn from both John's mistakes and his massive successes. What a great example of a "hand up" not a "hand out!" Thank you, John, for being such a great guy and such a fantastic inspiration and example!"*

—Leesa Clark-Price
SR. VP Statue of Responsibility Foundation

(1940s) Our apartment above Ralabate's grocery store

1946: As a toddler in Buffalo, NY

1947: John with family (note all deceased)
Back row, left: My mother's sister, my mother, my birthfather, and my Aunt Maria
Front row, left: My sister Jackie, myself and then Jim

Enjoying my dog Duchess on the couch at our place on Auburn Ave in 1955

My first set of snare drums, a gift from my brother-in-law, Danny, in 1956

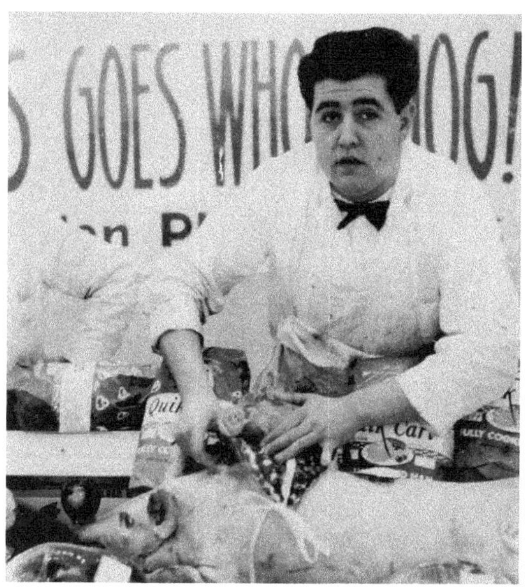

Training to be a meatcutter at Tops Market in 1963.

In 1967, I earned "Jaycee of the Year" - presented by Glenn Hackett

1978 trip to Bryce Canyon. Johnny 12 and Danny 7.

Johnny, 15 on his horse Pepper. He made it look easy! 1980

1981 Junior Posse! I loved sponsoring kids to develop their talents.

Once I left New York for the West, the whole world opened.

Crystal J. Stables became my third career for 7 years–and I broke even!

Celebration Bar - my first and last racehorse, 1983.

1984: August Houseboat Campsite on Lake Powell in 1984.

Snowmobiling with my sons, 1988.

Celebrating four generations of men in my family. Red proved you can choose your family.

My mom, Rose, with Red Robinette, the man who became my dad and life mentor.

Sugar cookie time with my four-year-old grandson, Tyson, 1990

One of several Hot Rockin 4th we put on in Ogden, plus Hot Country Nights.

Business and travel with Johnny. We didn't always agree, but we always made it work.

Road Trip to the Tetons. My Harley... my new horse made of steel.

Celebrating Hot Country Nights with my friend, Thurl Bailey.

Scuba Diving becomes my new passion

In 2024, I was inducted into the Pickleball Hall of Fame for years of growth and service to the sport.

Thurl and I in "Get Out the Vote!" 2024. (He's just a *little* taller than me.)

I was deeply honored when accepting the 2024 Pickleball Hall of Fame award to have my family present.

Truly enjoying my wedding day, 2026.

February 27, 2026 Marrying René, my best friend and love of my life!

www.ingramcontent.com/pod-product-compliance
Ingram Content Group UK Ltd.
Pitfield, Milton Keynes, MK11 3LW, UK
UKHW021908190726
13853UKWH00002B/564